MW01098225

# TALES OF THE
# WEIRRD

*by the same author*

Sigmund Freud
I. Leonardo
Between the Eyes
The Complete Alice and the Hunting of the Snark
(Lewis Carroll)
The Big I Am

for Derek Hoad
Artist and Artisan, who taught me
something I could never learn

Thanks must go to Ian Craig who art-directed this book into monumental
shape in characteristically masterly fashion, the wizard who magically cajoles
all my unmeasured lines to suit a plan of tender persuasion.

And thanks to Pascal Cariss, my editor, whose exquisite name belies an
uncompromising ability to hack the mannerist nineteenth-century prose
to bits in a heartfelt attempt to make it fit – and still make sense.

And, of course, to Tom Maschler, faithful defender of all my literary
efforts, who will insist on arguing about the title!! Bless you, Tom.

Frank Lentin (*who graces the front cover of this compendium*) had three legs. His third limb was the only part of a twin to be born with him, in Rosolini, Sicily, in 1889. It was not amputated at birth due to spinal complications, and Frank learned to live with his third leg quite successfully as a circus performer, throughout his life being billed as the 'Man with Two Dicks', though this was believed to be merely the result of entrepreneurial zeal.

He had a club foot and a small hint of a foot growing from the third leg. His two normal legs were in fact of slightly different lengths, thirty-nine inches and thirty-eight inches, respectively, and his third leg was only thirty-six inches long, which he used as a seat.

Though bitter in his childhood from the continued barrage of torment from his friends, he learned to live quite happily with his handicap when he saw others far worse off than himself in an institution.

When he bought shoes he chose two pairs, wore the right shoe on his third leg and gave the left shoe to a friend who had lost his right leg.

Throughout his life he was a kind and thoughtful man. In spite of a partial twin, for which he ate 15 per cent more than an average man in order to nourish it, he was never in two minds about anything.

A lady from Texas, Myrtle Corbin, however, went one better and was born with four legs. She had two normally proportioned legs and two legs the size of a child's, which dangled between the others, and wore matching shoes and socks. She too worked for circuses and, it was claimed, had two vaginas – and gave birth to three children from one 'body', and two from the other. She was married only once but her husband was never charged with bigamy.

# TALES OF THE
# WEIRRD

*Ralph Steadman*

FIREFLY BOOKS

# A Firefly Book

Published by Firefly Books Ltd., 2002

Copyright © 1990 Ralph Steadman

A few of the drawings in this book were first published in *Ambit* magazine.

All rights reserved. No part of this publication may be reproduced, stored in a retrieval system or transmitted in any form or by any means, electronic, mechanical, photocopying, recording or otherwise, without the prior written permission of the Publisher.

First Printing

National Library of Canada Cataloguing in Publication Data

Steadman, Ralph
  Tales of the weirrd [sic]

ISBN 1-55297-644-0

1. Eccentrics and eccentricities—Caricatures and cartoons.
2. Eccentrics and eccentricities—History.  3. Entertainers—Caricatures and cartoons.
4. Entertainers—History.  I. Title.
II. Title: Tales of the weird.  III. Title: Tales of the weirrd.

PN1583.S69 2002       741.5'942       C2002-900756-9

Publisher Cataloging-in-Publication Data (U.S.)

Steadman, Ralph.
  Tales of the weirrd / Ralph Steadman.
[112] p. :  ill. , photos. (some col.) ;   cm.
Originally published: London: Jonathan Cape, 1990.
Summary: An illustrated compendium of grotesques, odd people, imposters and eccentric people from 19th century.
ISBN 1-55297-644-0 (pbk.)
1. Eccentrics and eccentricities—19th century — Biography.  2. Impostors and imposture—19th century—Biography.  I. Title.
920.02 21     CIP     CT9990.S743 2002

Published in Canada in 2002 by
Firefly Books Ltd.
3680 Victoria Park Avenue
Toronto, Ontario M2H 3K1

Published in the United States in 2002 by
Firefly Books (U.S.) Inc.
P.O. Box 1338, Ellicott Station
Buffalo, New York 14205

Design: Christine Gilham based on an original design by Ian Craig

Printed and bound in Canada by
Friesens
Altona, Manitoba

# CONTENTS

*This —* — *and THIS —*

*— is a Normal MAN* *— is a Normal WOMAN*

*This —* *— and THIS —*

*— is an another Normal MAN* *is another Normal WOMAN*

*and again — THIS —* *— and yet again — THIS*

*— is a Normal MAN* *is a very Normal WOMAN.*

Therefore, the rest of us are WEIRD

# Introduction

Genuine Weirdness is a rare quality. To be truly weird demands character and a wanton disregard for the social mores of the day.

Strangely, it is not in the past century that the truly weird have emerged, even though we have witnessed mind-warping changes and can expect many more in the new millennium. The changes we have witnessed have not come about to make us all different, to help us find ourselves and realize our own identities. On the contrary, it seems that the essence of movement and change in the past century has had more to do with the control of difference, the standardization of mankind to satisfy a universal desire for sameness. Twentieth-century political ideologies have sought only to free us from one tyranny, and impose another more ruthless and more regulated tyranny upon us whose methods raze differences to the ground. The abnormal is treated with a general social disgust, as though human dignity had more to do with "neat front lawns" than the spirit and courage within our troubled minds.

Today, ideologies are structures into which people are systematically packed. Traditionally, ideologies were considered to be ideals fired with reason, rationalizing the best in us, the finest, our greatest hopes and aspirations. The Renaissance kindled the rebirth of Humanism through the arts and philosophic reflection, and stands as an example, a yardstick which still commands respect.

Ideologies of the twentieth century are nineteenth-century social dreams gone wrong, re-structured into practical systems to deny the individual. They have been exposed as euphemisms hiding terrifying crimes – the purging of millions of lives in the name of common goals – lowest common denominators masquerading as brave new worlds, the last refuge of a Utopian sleaze.

Though eccentricity was rife, the Victorians were not without blame in their denial of self and the individual. The respectable, the noble and the regal hid the shame of abnormality behind locked doors in remote rooms, treating such blighted wretches far worse that animals, as though a congenital defect was a curse to be vilified, along with its carrier, and not a human being with feelings to be nurtured and cared for.

Perhaps those who escaped such treatment due to circumstances of birth within a socially inferior section of society were luckier, for the afflicted could be displayed proudly as prized sideshow specimens for which money could be charged, even fortunes made. There was, after all, human contact and in many cases an admiration and sense of awe at the weirdness displayed before a credulous public. Some inbred mutants lived lives of luxury as court favourites, using their charm and their guile to win hearts and be accepted on equal terms, or at least as engaging novelties, which gave them some kind of decent life.

In our time, these physical and mental abnormalities are viewed with an awkward repugnance and an embarrassment, for we can neither display such things for profit, shut them away in towers, nor live comfortably with them side by side in a streamlined society which prizes the ordinary, the conventional and the unobtrusive. We have civilized ourselves to be decent and law-abiding and uncompassionate. We are not caring for the growing numbers of "normal inadequates" who cannot absorb the stresses of our highly developed and bureaucratic lifestyle.

What chance for a being who is truly weird? If all mankind were weird maybe the normal would look strange.

In 1969 I happened upon a book published in 1869 by Reeves and Turner, 196 Strand, London. It is a collection of Wonderful Characters written about by Henry Wilson and James Caulfield. For twenty years I have considered it a book to be re-made and the characters portrayed as they might have been. Gradually, the revised collection emerged and recently I finished it and decided to use the same enchanting text which is so steeped in the turn of phrase of mid-Victorian England. I could do no better, but I have included other weird and wonderful characters found elsewhere. I have given my own account of their lives. The subjects are to be found in several books, but in that context more as a collection of sideshow curiosities from the *Guinness Book of Records* or *Ripley's Believe It or Not*.

This is a book of characters who inspired drawings I could not have imagined without the proof of their one-time existence.

I resisted including twentieth-century characters. With a few exceptions, people of a genuinely unusual appearance ceased to exist professionally with the passing of silent movies, crowned by Tod Browning's 1933 masterpiece, *Freaks*. Today, weirdness is recreated in special-effects workshops tailor-made to suit a film, sometimes ingenious, sometimes pathetic but, weirdly, always in demand.

With the passage of time between us and the truly weird of long ago we can allow a certain fantasy to surround these special beings. Maybe the facts have been changed or embellished with the telling, which is the essence of a good story anyway. We can treat them as fairy tales. It also allows me to view them objectively without remorse, and with candour and sometimes humour. Look upon my effort as a graphic reincarnation of their kind viewed from a place in history where people have cancelled out the prospect that difference can be cultivated and regarded as a virtue.

# Francis Battalia

## The Stone-Eater

In 1641 Hollar etched a plate of Francis Battalia, an Italian, who is said to have eaten half a peck of stones a day. Respecting this individual, Dr. Bulwer, in his *Artificial Changeling*, relates that he saw him in London when he was about thirty years of age; that he was born with two stones in one hand and one in the other. As soon as he was born, having the breast offered him, he refused to suck, and when they would have fed him with pap, he utterly rejected that also. Whereupon, the midwife and nurse entering into consideration of the strangeness of his birth and refusal of all kind of nourishment, consulted with some physicians what they should do in this case. They, when they saw the infant reject all that they could contrive for nourishment, told the women they thought that the child brought its meat with it into the world, and that it was to be nourished with stones; whereupon they desired the nurse to give him one stone in a little drink, which he very readily took into his mouth and swallowed down. When he had swallowed all the three stones and began to want his hard-meat, the physicians advised the nurse to get some small pebbles, as like those which he was born with as they could, with which kind of nourishment he was brought up, and on which he continued to subsist in manhood. Dr. Bulwer thus describes his manner of feeding: "His manner is to put three or four stones into a spoon, and so putting them into his mouth together, he swallows them all down one after another; then (first spitting) he drinks a glass of beer after them. He devours about half a peck of these stones every day, and when he chinks upon his stomach, or shakes his body, you may hear the stones rattle as if they were in a sack, all which in twenty-four hours are resolved. Once in three weeks he voids a great quantity of sand, after which he has a fresh appetite for these stones, as we have for our victuals, and by these, with a cup of beer, and a pipe of tobacco, he has his whole subsistence. He has attempted to eat meat and bread, broth and milk, and such kind of food, upon which other mortals commonly live; but he could never brook any, neither would they stay with him to do him any good. He is a black, swartish little fellow, active and strong enough, and has been a soldier in Ireland, where he made great use of this property; for, having the advantage of this strange way of alimony, he sold his allowance of food sometimes at high rates. At Limerick he sold a sixpenny loaf and two-penny worth of cheese for twelve shillings and sixpence. It seems the fellow when he first came out was suspected to be an imposter, and was, by command of the State, shut up for a month, with the allowance of two pots of beer and half an ounce of tobacco every day, but was afterwards acquitted from all suspicion and deceit." ➤

Francis BATTALIA
The STONE EATER

Ralph STEADman 89.

9

# De Hightrehight, John Cummings and Cliquot
## Fire-Eaters and Sword-Swallowers

It seems at first sight difficult to account for the strange phenomenon of a human and perishable creature eating red-hot coals, taken indiscriminately out of a large fire; broiling steaks upon his tongue; swallowing huge draughts of liquid fire as greedily as a country squire does roast beef and strong beer. How can that element which we are told is ultimately to devour all things, be devoured itself, as familiar diet, by a mortal man?

Sir Henry Wotton, a close friend of Mr. John Donne, in a letter to one of his correspondents, dated June 3rd, 1633, speaks of "a strange thing to be seen in London for a couple of pence, which I know not I should call a piece of art or nature. It is an Englishman like some swabber of a ship come from the Indies, where he has learned to eat fire as familiarly as ever I saw any eat cakes, even whole glowing brands, which he will crash with his teeth, and swallow. I believe he hath been hard famished in the Terra de Fuego, on the South of the Magellan strait."

One of the amusements of 1718 was the juggling exhibition of a fire-eater, whose name was De Hightrehight, a native of the valley of Annivi, in Savoy, among the Alps that divide Italy from Switzerland. This tremendous person ate burning coals, chewed flaming brimstone, and swallowed it; licked a red-hot poker; placed a red-hot heater on his tongue; suffered them to be blown, and broiled meat on them; ate melted pitch, brimstone, bees'-wax, sealing-wax and resin, with a spoon; and to complete the business, he performed all these marvels five times a day, at the Duke of Marlborough's Head, in Fleet Street, for the trifling sums of 2s 6d., 1s 6d., and 1s. Master Hightrehight had the honour of exhibiting before Louis XIV, the Kaiser, the King of Sicily, the Doge of Venice, and an infinite number of princes and nobles – including the Prince of Wales, who had nearly lost that inconceivable pleasure by the envious interposition of the Inquisition at Bologna and Piedmont, which Holy Office seemed inclined to try their mode of burning on his body, leaving to him the care of resisting the flames, and rendering them harmless. He was, however, preserved from the unwelcome ordeal by the interference of the Duchess Royal Regent of Savoy, and the Marquis Bentivoglio.

In June, 1799, *John Cummings*, an American sailor, aged about twenty-three, having seen a man near Havre-de-Grace amuse the crowd of people by pretending to swallow clasp-knives, returned on board and told his shipmates what he had seen, and being rather fresh with liquor, boasted he could swallow knives as well as the Frenchman. Being pressed to do it, he did not like to go against his word, and having a good supply of grog inwardly, he took his own pocket-knife, and on trying to swallow it, it slipped down his throat with great ease, and by the assistance of some drink was conveyed into his stomach. The spectators, however, were not satisfied with one experiment, and asked the operator whether he could

swallow more? His answer was – 'All the knives on board ship'; upon which three knives were immediately produced, which were swallowed in the same way as the former; and by this bold attempt of a drunken man, the company was well entertained for that night.

After this extraordinary performance, he thought no more of swallowing knives for the next six years. In March, 1805, being then at Boston, in America, he was one day tempted, while drinking with a party of sailors, to boast of his former exploits, adding that he was the same man still, and ready to repeat his performance. A small knife was thereupon produced, which he instantly swallowed. In the course of the evening he swallowed five more. The next morning crowds of visitors came to see him; and in the course of that day, he was induced to swallow eight knives more, making in all fourteen! He, however, paid dearly for this frolic. He was seized with constant vomiting and pain in his stomach; but, as he related, between that time and the 28th of the following month, he got rid of the whole of his cargo. At Spithead, December 4th, in the same year, he was challenged to repeat his feats, and 'disdaining to be worse than his word', in the course of the evening he swallowed five knives. The ship's company, next morning, expressed a great desire to see him repeat the performance, and he compiled with his usual readiness; and by the encouragement of the people, and the assistance of good grog, he swallowed that day nine clasp-knives, some of which were very large; and he was afterwards assured by the spectators that he had swallowed four more; which, however, he declared he knew nothing about, being, no doubt, at this period of the business too much intoxicated to have any recollection of what was passing. This, however, is the last performance recorded; it made a total of at least thirty-five knives swallowed at different times and the last attempt ultimately put an end to his existence. On the following 6th December he became much indisposed; and after various applications, about three months afterwards he felt, as he expressed himself, the knives 'dropping down his bowels.' He continued dreadfully ill. In 1807 he was in Guys Hospital, under Dr. Babington; and he there continued, intervals excepted, under that physician, and afterwards under Dr. Curry, till March, 1809. After gradually and miserably sunk under his suffering, he then died, in a state of extreme emaciation.

*Cliquot*, a famous sword-swallower, turned out to be none other than Fred McLane, a completely unknown nobody from a wealthy Chicago family. However, he perfected a sword-swallowing act of great ingenuity.

As a runaway youngster he watched a circus performer swallow a machete in Buenos Aires. He was fired with an ambition to do the same and practiced endlessly with lengths of copper wire until he overcame the unpleasant nausea and choking that most of us experience when something foreign touches the back of the throat.

Gradually he learned to swallow anything from cavalry swords to pocket watches which with the aid of a stethoscope could be heard ticking inside him. Another trick of Cliquot's was to swallow an electric light bulb attached to a battery which would light up the bulb inside him.

His greatest trick, however, was to swallow a sword weighted down with heavy dumbbells weighing a total of 76 lbs, which surprisingly never pierced his insides. Getting the contraption down inside him was no problem whatsoever, but regurgitation proved an overdemanding task night after night and left him an exhausted and broken man and finished him completely when during one performance his stage assistant walked off halfway through the act following a backstage argument. ✺

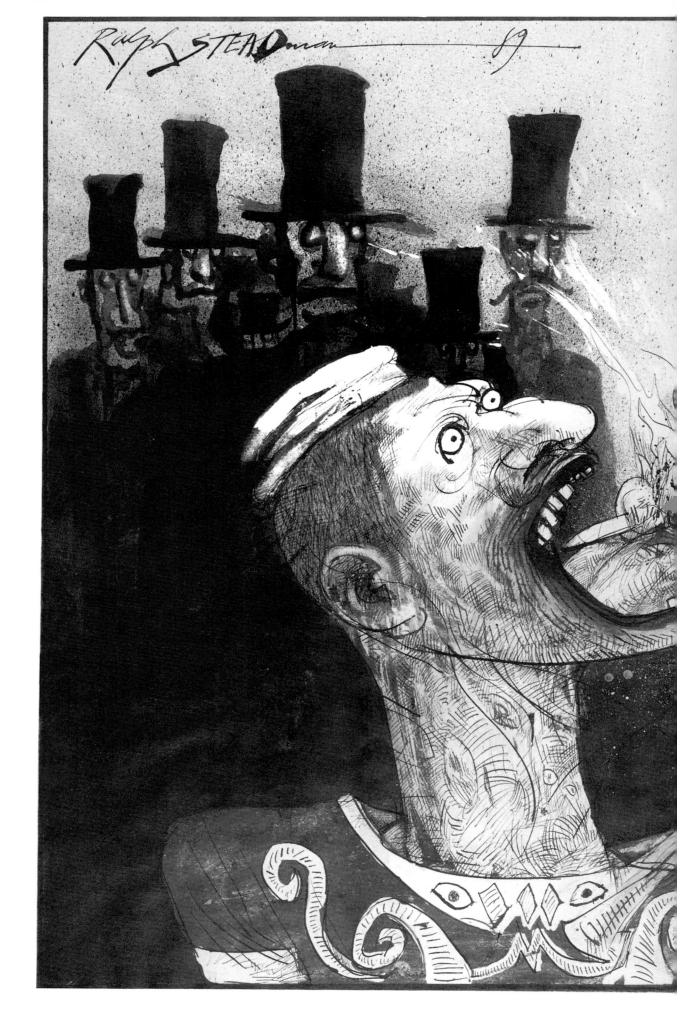

13

# John Broughton

## A Notorious Pugilist

John Broughton, who has been styled 'the founder of the British School of Boxing', was born in 1704, and for many years followed the profession of a waterman, and was the first man who won Dogget's Coat and a badge, which is rowed for annually, on the first of August. He, however, abandoned his wherry for the more profitable, though less honourable, employment of pugilism.

About the middle of the last century boxing began to obtain notoriety, through the encouragement afforded by some gambling and vitiated noblemen, and others, headed by the well-known Duke of Cumberland, who drew in their train numbers of weak-minded and dissipated persons, who are always found ready to mix among nobility, for the honour of boasting an acquaintance with lords and dukes.

About this time one George Taylor erected a booth at Tottenham Court, where he invited the professors of the art to display their skill, and the public to be present at its exhibition. The entrance-money at times amounted to £100 or £150; two-thirds of which were generally given to the champion, and the remaining third to the loser; though sometimes, by an express agreement of the parties, the money was shared alike between the conqueror and the conquered. Taylor's booth being complained of as inconvenient, Broughton, who was then rising into note as the first bruiser in London, was prevailed on to build a place better adapted for such exhibitions, near Oxford Street, which was opened on the 10th March, 1743, under the name of 'Broughton's New Amphitheatre'.

But the foundation of the 'British School of Boxing', for which Broughton is notorious, was his opening an academy which was first announced in the *Daily Advertiser*, February 1st, 1747: 'Mr. Broughton proposes, with proper assistance, to open an academy at his house, in the Haymarket, for the instruction of those who are willing to be initiated in the majesty of boxing, where the whole theory and practice of that truly British art, with all the various stops, blows, cross-buttocks, etc., incident to the combatants, will be fully taught and explained; and, that persons of quality and distinction may not be debarred from entering into a course of those lectures, they will be given with the utmost tenderness and regard to the delicacy of the frame and constitution of the pupil, for which reason muffles (boxing gloves) are provided, that will effectually secure them from the inconvenience of black eyes, broken jaws, and bloody noses.'

This invitation had the desired effect; the academy was numerously attended, and was a source of great profit to its proprietor.

Broughton, after fighting several years, and maintaining his ascendancy, was at length vanquished by Slack, in April, 1750, at Broughton's Amphitheatre. Some thousands were lost on the unexpected defeat; and nearly £150 was taken at the door, besides many tickets being sold at a guinea and a half each, all of which went to Slack, who is supposed to have gained nearly £600 by his victory. After this defeat Broughton never fought again; and his amphitheatre was shortly after shut up. ✳

John BROUGHTON
A Notorious Pugilist

# Bertholde

## Prime Minister to Alboinus

Though nature had been unfavourable to this wonderful character with respect to his body, she had recompensed him by the subtlety, the agreeableness and the solidity of the mind she had united to it. This advantage, infinitely more precious than all others, raised him from being a simple and mean peasant, to be the favourite of a great prince, and happily extricated him out of all the snares and dangers that had been laid for him.

Bertholde had a large head, as round as a foot-ball, adorned with red hair very strait, and which had a great resemblance to the bristles of a hog; an extremely short forehead, furrowed with wrinkles; two little blear eyes, edged round with a border of bright carnation, and overshadowed by a pair of large eyebrows, which, upon occasion, might be made use of as brushes; a flat nose, resembling an extinguisher, a wide mouth, from which proceeded two long crooked teeth, not unlike the tusks of a boar, and pointing to a pair of ears, like those which formerly belonged to Midas; a lip of a monstrous thickness, which hung down on a chin, that seemed to sink under the load of a beard, thick, strait and bristly; a very short neck, which nature had adorned with a kind of necklace, formed of ten or twelve small wrens. The rest of his body was perfectly in keeping with the grotesque appearance of his visage; so that from head to foot, he was a kind of monster, who, by his deformity, and the hair with which he was covered, had a greater resemblance to a bear half licked into form, than to a human creature.

In his maturity Bertholde went to Verona, where Alboin, the first king of the Lombards, after having conquered the greatest part of Italy, kept his court. Chance conducted Bertholde to the palace of this prince, and as he had heard of his goodness but never seen him, he resolved to pay the prince a visit. In this age, the gates of palaces were not yet blocked up with guards, everyone had free access to lay his grievances before the throne.

Though a peasant, though a clown, though disgraced by nature, reason dictated to him that all men were formed by the same hand, and created in perfect equality; he, therefore, thought there was no person on earth with whom he might not be allowed to converse familiarly.

In consequence of this principle, he entered the palace without any conductor, marched up stairs, traversed the apartments, and entered into that in which the king was surrounded by his courtiers, who were conversing with him in a respectful posture, and laughing; but how great was their astonishment to see Bertholde walk in with his hat on his head, and, without speaking a word, come boldly up to them, and seat himself by the side of the king, on a chair,

which they, out of respect, had left empty! Surprised at this rusticity, and more still at his grotesque appearance, they stood immovable at the view of this second Aesop, whose mean dress was very suitable to his deformity. From this rustic behaviour, the king easily guessed that he was one whom curiosity had brought to his court. And as he had learned from experience, that nature sometimes hides her treasure under the most unpromising form, he resolved to have a familiar conversation with him, and for a few minutes, in complaisance to the clown, to forget his own grandeur and dignity. 'Who are you?' cried the prince to Bertholde: 'How did you come into the world? What is your country?' – 'I am a man,' replied the peasant; 'I came into the world in the manner Providence sent me, and the world itself is my country.'

The king then asked him several questions, which had not the least connection with each other – a trial of wit, which in those days was much used at the courts of sovereign princes. And this is the substance of the discourse, as it is preserved in the ancient records of the country. 'What thing is that which flies the swiftest?' cried the monarch. 'Thought,' answered Bertholde. 'What is the gulf that is never filled?' 'The avarice of the miser.' 'What is most hateful in young people?' – 'Self-conceit, because it makes them incorrigible.' 'What is most ridiculous in the old?' – 'Love.' 'Who are most lavish of their caresses?' – 'Those who intend to deceive us, and those who have already done it.' 'What are the things most dangerous in a house?' – 'A wicked wife, and the tongue of a servant.' 'What is the husband's most incurable disease? – 'The infidelity of his wife.' 'What way will you take to bring water into a sieve?' – 'I'll stay till it is frozen.' 'How will you catch a hare without running?' – 'I will wait till I find her on the spit.'

The king was astonished at the readiness with which he answered these questions; and to let him see his satisfaction, promised to give him anything he could desire. 'I defy you,' replied Bertholde, bluntly. 'How so?' replied his majesty; 'do you doubt my good will?' – 'No; but I aspire after what you do not possess, and consequently cannot give to me.' 'And what is this precious thing that I do not possess?' – 'Happiness, which was never in the power of kings, who enjoy less of it than the rest of mankind.' 'How! am I not happy on so elevated a throne?' – 'Yes, you are, if the happiness of a man consists in the height of his seat.' 'Do you see these lords and gentlemen that are continually about me, would they be always ready to obey me, if they were not convinced of my power?' – 'And do you not see, in your turn, that there are as many crows, waiting to devour a carcase, and who, to prevent its seeing their designs, begin by picking out its eyes.' 'Well said, but all this does not hinder me from shining in the midst of them, as the sun among the stars.' – 'True, but tell me, shining sun, how many eclipses you are obliged to suffer in a year?' 'Why do you put this questions?' - 'Because the continual flattery of these gentlemen will raise a cloud that must darken your understanding.' 'On this foot, then, you would not be courtier?' – 'Miserable as I am, I should be sorry to be placed in the rank of slaves; besides, I am neither knave, traitor, nor liar, and consequently have not the necessary qualities for succeeding in this fine employment.' 'What are you then to seek for at my court?' – 'What I have not been able to find there; for I had imagined a king to be as much above other men, as a steeple is above common houses; but I have soon found, that I have honoured them more than they deserve.'

Of all the virtues, those of frankness and sincerity have been in every age least recompensed in a court. This Bertholde experienced; for the king, shocked at the little regard he expresses for his person, told him, that if he was unwilling to be turned out in an ignominious manner, he must leave the palace immediately. He obeyed, but as he was going, said, with an air of gaiety, that he was of the nature of flies, which the more you attempt to drive away,

the more obstinately are they bent on their return. 'I permit you to return like them,' cried the monarch, 'provided you bring them along with you; but if you appear without them, you shall forfeit your head.' – 'Agreed,' replied the peasant; 'to do this I will only take a step to our village.' The king gave his consent, and Bertholde hasted away. The monarch did not doubt of his keeping his word; but had a great curiosity to see in what manner he would perform it, and the clown soon satisfied him: for he had no sooner reached the village, than running to a stable belonging to one of his brothers, he took out an old ass, whose back and buttocks had lost the friendly covering of a sound skin, and mounting on his back, turned again to Verona, accompanied by an infinite number of flies riding behind him, and in this equipage arrived at the palace; when commending the fidelity with which they had stuck to the beast, and attending him all the way, he told the king, that he had kept his promise; and Alboin, pleased with his stratagem, soon conceived such an idea of his abilities, that he imagined he might be useful to him, in helping him to disentangle the intricacies of government, and therefore gave him free leave to stay at court.

He was later made prime minister, and under his influence the reign of this prince was happy, and his people enjoyed all the happiness they could reasonably desire. 

BERTHOLDE
Prime Minister to
ALBOINUS.
King of LOMBARDY

# Matthew Buchinger

## The Little Man of Nuremberg

O f all the imperfect beings brought into the world, few can challenge, for mental and acquired endowments, anything like a comparison to vie with this truly extraordinary little man. Matthew Buchinger was a native of Nuremberg, in Germany, where he was born June 2nd, 1674, without hands, feet, legs or thighs; in short, he was little more than the trunk of a man, saving two excrescences growing from the shoulder-blades, more resembling fins of a fish than arms of a man. He was the last of nine children, by one father and mother, viz., eight sons and one daughter. After arriving at the age of maturity, from the singularity of his case, and the extraordinary abilities he possessed, he attracted the notice and attentions of all persons, of whatever rank in life, to whom he was occasionally introduced.

It does not appear, by any account extant, that his parents exhibited him at any time for the purpose of emolument, but that the whole of his time must have been employed in study and practice, to attain the wonderful perfection he arrived at in drawing, and his performance on various musical instruments; he played the flute, the bagpipe, dulcimer, and trumpet, not in the manner of general amateurs, but in the style of a finished master. He likewise possessed great mechanical powers, and conceived the design of constructing machines to play on all sort of musical instruments.

If nature played the niggard in one respect with him, she amply repaid the deficiency by endowments that those blessed with perfect limbs could seldom achieve. He greatly distinguished himself by beautiful writing, drawing

MR. MATHEW BUCHINGER
The Little Man of Nuremberg

Ralph Steadman

coats of arms, sketches of portraits, history, landscapes, etc., most of which were executed in Indian ink, with a pen, emulating in perfection the finest and most finished engraving. He was well skilled in most games of chance, nor could the most experienced gamester or juggler obtain the least advantage at any tricks, or game, with cards or dice.

He used to perform before company, to whom he was exhibited, various tricks with cups and balls, corn, and living birds; and could play at skittles and nine-pins with great dexterity; shave himself with perfect ease and do many other things equally surprising in a person so deficient, and mutilated by nature. His writings and sketches of figures, landscapes, etc., were by no means uncommon, though curious; it being customary, with most persons who went to see him, to purchase something or other of his performance; and as he was always employed in writing or drawing, he carried on a very successful trade, which, together with the money he obtained by exhibiting himself, enabled him to support himself and family in a very genteel manner. Mr. Herbert, of Cheshunt, editor of *Ames's History of Printing*, had many curious specimens of

Buchinger's writing and drawing, the most extraordinary of which was his own portrait, exquisitely done on vellum, in which he most ingeniously contrived to insert, in the flowing curls of the wig, the 27th, 121st, 128th, 140th, 149th, and 150th Psalms, together with the Lord's Prayer, most beautifully and fairly written. Mr. Isaac Herbert, son of the former, while carrying on the business of a bookseller in Pall Mall, cause this portrait to be engraved, for which he paid Mr. Harding fifty guineas.Buchinger was married four times, and had eleven children, viz., one by his first wife, three by his second, six by his third, and one by his last. One of his wives was in the habit of treating him extremely ill, frequently beating him and otherwise insulting him, which for a long time he very patiently put up with; but once his anger was so much roused, that he sprang upon her like fury, got her down, and buffeted her with this stumps within an inch of her life; nor would he suffer her to rise until she promised amendment in future, which it seems she prudently adopted, through fear of another thrashing.

Mr. Buchinger was but twenty-nine inches in height. He died in 1722.  ✳

# Miss Whitehead

## The Bank Nun

Miss Sarah Whitehead, of Bank notoriety, was called by the clerks of that establishment the Bank Nun, from the peculiarity of her dress, which was really emblematic of her mind.

Her brother had held a situation as clerk in the Bank, which he filled for some years with much satisfaction to his employers; but being rather too high-minded for his income, he commenced dabbling in the stocks, hoping thereby to increase his means, if not to make a splendid fortune.

This proceeding, however, reached the ears of the directors, who, unwilling to enforce the penalty of such a violation of their rules and orders, only rebuked him, accompanying it with an assurance, that if continued, his discharge was certain. This check was too much for his pride to brook, and after a few weeks he sent in his resignation. This step gave some offence to his real friends, but as he persevered in the business of stock-jobbing, and appeared to be flourishing, they thought it would turn out for the best; but unfortunately, it proved his ruin. The higher he rose upon the unsubstantial ladder of speculation the more means he required for his extravagances. High company dazzled his imagination, and capricious fortune turning her back upon him, the bubble of his golden dream burst.

Hungry creditors, who miscalculated on the stability of their betters, became clamorous for their accounts. Want planted a withering finger where luxury had before revelled. Despair seized him, and, hurried on by the fiends, he associated himself with the notorious Roberts. With this man poor Whitehead had sundry unlawful dealings, but all proved abortive, for in an unpropitious hour he committed a forgery for a large amount in the 'Old Navy Fives', and the transaction being discovered through the house of Roberts, Curtis and Company, he was prosecuted at the Old Bailey. Death was pronounced to be his doom, and he was conveyed to the condemned cell to ruminate upon that conduct which it was now too late to remedy.

The whole of this unfortunate affair was carefully concealed from his sister; and poor Sarah was removed to the house of a friend in Wine Office Court, Fleet Street, in order that she should not hear the knell of St. Sepulchre's Church toll his departure.

His long absence began to prey upon her spirits, and, like the rose plucked from its parent stems, she lost her beauty and began to droop. She had felt the force of unrequited love, which assisted the melancholy that now took possession of her. Unable to account for his continued absence from home, and fancying that he had formed a matrimonial alliance, she one day, without the

knowledge of her friends, proceeded to the bank to satisfy her suspicions, when an unthinking fellow clerk informed her of his crime and ignominious death. The horrible intelligence was too much for her affectionate mind: she

Miss Whitehead
The Bank Nun.

uttered not a word, shed not a tear; but stood pale and motionless as marble. This shock entirely overturned her mind; and the amiable Sarah, just bursting forth in all her prime of womanhood and beauty, having been ripened by hardly twenty summers, became an utter wreck.

In a dress of sable, with painted face, and head enveloped with a sort of coronet fancifully decked out with streamers of black crape, and reticule hung on her arm, she daily attended at the Bank, where she continued loitering about for hours, waiting for her brother, under the belief

that he was still employed in the establishment. Being in decayed circumstances, the governors of the Bank frequently presented her with sums of money in compliment to her misfortunes; and the clerks were equally mindful of her situation. She imbibed a peculiar impression, emanating, no doubt, from early dreams of pride, that the directors of the Bank kept her out of immense sums of money, which upon some occasions worked her up to insult her benefactors by making violent demands upon them for it, during the hours of business, and obliged them, however painful it might be to their own feelings, to interdict her admission to any part of the building. This, however, was reserved but for a time. Upon one occasion she attacked Baron Rothschild upon the Stock Exchange, in the midst of his business, and after calling him a villain and a robber, telling him he had defrauded her of her fortune, demanded the £2,000 he owed her; upon which, after casting his eyes upon her for a moment, he took half a crown from his waistcoat pocket, and giving it to her, said, 'There, then, take that, and don't bother me now; I'll give you the other half tomorrow,' upon which she thanked him and went away.

She broke very fast, and at length, some time before her death, discontinued altogether her visits to the Bank. ✻

# Joseph Clark

## The Posture Master

This man was a very extraordinary posture master who reside in Pall Mall. Though well made, and rather gross than thin, he exhibited, in a most natural manner, almost every species of deformity and dislocation. He frequently diverted himself with the tailors, by sending for one of them to take measure of him, and would so contrive it as to have a most immoderate rising in one of the shoulders: when the clothes were brought home, and tried upon him, the deformity was removed into the other shoulder; upon which the tailor asked pardon for the mistake, and altered the garment as expeditiously as possible, but, upon a third trial, he found him perfectly free from blemish about the shoulders, though an unfortunate lump appeared upon his back. In short, this wandering tumour puzzled all the workmen about town, who found it impossible to accommodate so changeable a customer. He dislocated the vertebrae of his back, and other parts of the body, in such a manner that Molins, the famous surgeon, before whom he appeared as a patient, was shocked at the sight, and would not even attempt his cure. He often passed for a cripple among persons with whom he had been in company but a few minutes before. Upon these occasions he would not only change the position of his limbs, but entirely alter the figure of his countenance. The powers of his face were more extraordinary than the flexibility of his body. He would assume all the uncouth grimaces that he saw at a Quakers' meeting, the theatre, or any other public place. He died about the beginning of King William's reign, as it appears from Evelyn's *Numismata* that he was not living in 1697.

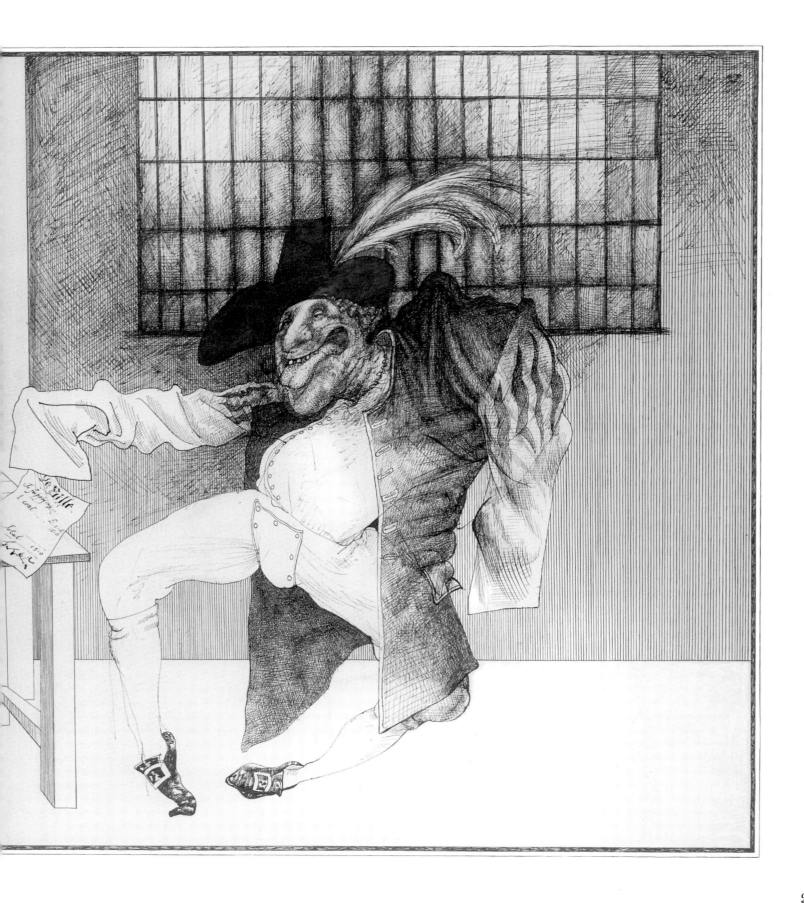

# Nathaniel Bentley
## The Well-Known 'Dirty Dick'

Nathaniel Bentley, late the proprietor of a hardware shop in Leadenhall Street, known by the characteristic appellation of the Dirty Warehouse, and himself distinguished by that of Dirty Dick, was the son of a gentleman of the same name, who carried on the same business in those premises. The elder Bentley, being of a tyrannical disposition, treated him, as well as his servants, in the most unreasonable manner, in consequence of which young Bentley ran away from his father, and was absent several years; during which time it is supposed that he contracted that peculiar turn of mind which afterwards manifested itself in such an eccentric manner.

Previous to the death of his father, and for some years after that event, young Bentley was called the beau of Leadenhall Street, and was seen at all public places dressed as a man of fashion. At this period his favourite suit was blue and silver; his hair adopted the highest style of fashionable extravagance.

At what time he began to assume his extraordinary appearance is uncertain. Though he still attended at masquerades, assemblies, and other public places, in the most elegant attire, yet his appearance at home was such as to fully justify the above epitaph.

Bentley's house, which was of a large size, had originally a front of white plaster, which time had converted into a dingy black. Its outside perfectly corresponded with the interior. The windows were literally as black, and covered as thickly with dirt and smoke, as the back of a chimney which has not been swept for many years. Of the windows, scarcely a pane was left whole, to remedy which several of the window shutters long remained unopened, and the other vacancies were repaired with japanned waiters, and tea-trays, which were always chained to the window frames. Though this method of proceeding may appear to have arisen from parsimony, yet notoriety, rather than avarice, seemed to be his ruling principle. By the adoption of this dirty system he found, by experience, that he excited much curiosity, and attracted considerable notice. Several of this neighbours, especially those on the opposite side of the street, frequently offered to defray the expense of painting and repairing the front of his house, but this he constantly refused, alleging that his shop was so well-known abroad, as well as at home, by the denomination of the Dirty Warehouse of Leadenhall Street, that to alter its appearance would ruin his trade with the Levant and other foreign parts.

He generally attended in his shop without a coat, while the remainder of his dress and his whole person exactly corresponded with the appearance of his warehouse. On returning from any place of public entertainment, his elegant attire was immediately thrown aside for this shop clothing, which he mended himself; and it was also said that he made no secret of washing and mending his own linen, and of purchasing his shoes at Rag-fair.

A gentlemen once venturing to give him some advice respecting the propriety of a little more attention to personal cleanliness, he replied, 'It is of no use, sir; if I wash my hands to-day they will be dirty again to-morrow.'

Latterly he did not go out more than once of twice in a year, on account of his being so tormented by the gaping multitude, who were all in uproar after him, that he was often obliged to have the assistance of the beadle, or a constable, to disperse them.

# Lord Rokeby
## Of Singular Eccentricity

Matthew Robinson Morris, eldest son of Sir Septimus Robinson, Knt., was born at his father's house at Mount Morris, in Horton, near Hythe, in the county of Kent, in the year 1712. As heir to a country gentleman of considerable property, he was not compelled to apply his abilities to the usual pursuit of a laborious profession; he enjoyed an introduction to the higher circles of life, and being possessed of the advantages of a liberal education, and accomplished manners, he united the studies of the scholar with the occupations of a gentleman, and divided his time very agreeably between Horton, London, Bath and Cambridge.

By the death of his father, in the second period in his parliamentary life, Mr. Robinson came into possession of the paternal estate. Mr. R. took the whole of this land into his own occupation as soon as possible; and nature, with his occupancy, began to resume her rights. The boundaries on his estate were soon only those which separated his land from that of his neighbours. Adieu to the use of gates or stiles in the interior: they were left to gradual decay; the soil was not disturbed by the labours of horse and man; the cattle had free liberty to stray wherever they pleased; the trees were no longer dishonoured by the axe of the woodman, the pollards strove to recover their pristine vigour, the uniformity of hedges and ditches gradually disappeared. The richest verdure clothed both hills and valleys, and the master of the mansion wandered freely in his grounds, enjoying his own independence and that of the brute creation around him.

The singularity of this taste excited naturally a great deal of curiosity, and, as usual, no small degree of censure. But, whatever may be objected on the score of profit, it is certain that the gain on the scale of picturesque beauty was, we might almost say, infinite. At the same time that nature resumed her rights over his fields, she took full possession of the master, and gave him the active use of his limbs. The family coach stirred not from its place to the day of his death: he seldom got into a chaise, and performed long journeys on foot. Naturally of a tender and a delicate constitution, he thus became hardened to all weathers, and enjoyed his faculties and spirits to the day of his death.

Lord Rokeby was a venerable man with a long beard, sallow complexion, furrows on his forehead, the traces of deep thinking, brow part of the head bald, from the hinder flowed long and lank locks of white hair, a white or blue flannel coat and waistcoat, and breeches, worsted stockings, and shoes tied with black strings. The ruffles at his wrist, and the frill sewed to his waistcoat, were the only linen about him. His body was rather bent, but till he was near his end, his pace was firm, and he was seen walking in this manner from his house to Hythe or back, or, which was more gratifying to his friends, when they first caught a view of the house, walking up and down the pavement before his door. 'How can this man be a lord?' said the vulgar. 'Would to God more lords were like this man!' said the man of sense. 'I wish we were all as attentive to good breeding!' said the man of fashion.

He never willingly omitted bathing a single day, and had made, for that purpose, a bathing-house of considerable length and breadth, glazed in front to a south-eastern aspect, and thatched at top.

A gentleman who happened to be in the neighbourhood of Mount Morris, resolved to procure a sight of this extraordinary character:

'He had just come out of the water, and was dressed in an old blue woolen coat, and pantaloons of the same colour. The upper part of his head was bald, but the hair of

his chin, which could not be concealed even by the posture he had assumed, made its appearance between his arms on his side. I immediately retired, and waited at a little distance until he awoke; when rising, he opened the door, darted through the thicket, accompanied by his dogs, and made directly for the house.'

His memory was prodigious. In conversation, if anything occurred which afforded room for difference of opinion, he would frequently run on the sudden to his library, bring back a folio or two, and point out the passage on which the whole depended. He was a great reader as well as a deep thinker, and preserved the use of his eyes to the last: for writing, he very frequently availed himself of the help of an amanuensis. In so singular a character, it is natural that persons little acquainted with it should make very erroneous conjectures. However, he was an excellent master and a good neighbour; just in all his dealings, of strict honour, firmly attached to the liberty of his country, of a most enlarged mind, a true free-thinker, and, with all the singularities in his dress and manners, he united to his love of nature and independence all the good qualities from which constitute a perfect gentleman.

From what has been already said, it appears that, independent of his beard, which reached to his waist, Lord Rokeby was a very singular character. He lived a considerable portion of his life in water, tempered by the rays of the sun, and traveled on foot at an age when people of his rank and fortune always indulged in a carriage. In the midst of a luxurious age he was abstemious both in eating and drinking, and attained to length of life without having recourse to the aid of medicine, and indeed with an utter contempt for the practitioners of physic. This he carried to such a length, that it is related, when a paroxysm was expected to come on, his lordship told his nephew that if he stayed he was welcome; but if, out of a false humanity, he should call in medical assistance, and it should accidentally happen that he was not killed by the doctor, he hoped he should have sufficient use of his hands and senses left to make a new will and disinherit him.

This truly patriotic nobleman expired at his seat in Kent, in the month of December, 1800, in the eighty-eighth year of his life.

# Toby
## A Begging Impostor

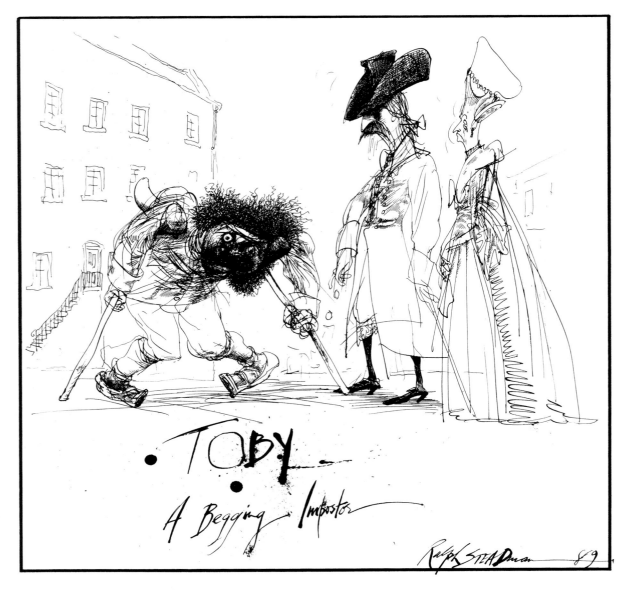

This impostor, whose real name is unknown, frequented the streets of London in the early part of the twentieth century and lived upon the credulity of the too charitable metropolis, in which place he was only known by the familiar appellation of Toby. He was a Negro, and during a passage from Bermuda to Memel, while on board a merchantman, lost all his toes; this accident was however, of great service, by rendering him an object of pity and compassion, during his daily perambulations.

This use of his own language was also of great help to him, in fixing the attention of passengers, and a great inducement to many to extend their charity to this apparently distressed stranger; indeed, he left no method untried to work upon the various dispositions of those he supplicated. Very often he would preach to the spectators gathered round him, and sometimes would amuse another sort of auditors with a song; and when begging, he always appeared almost bent double, as if with excessive pain and fatigue. But when his day's business was done, he laid aside all constraint and walked upright; and at the beggars' meeting there was not a more jovial member than he. From these midnight revels he adjourned to a miserable lodging, from which in the morning he again sallied forth in quest of those credulous persons, who will ever be found in so extensive a metropolis as London.

In this way passed many years of the life of Toby, until the indiscriminating hand of death snatched him from a state which he had so long abused and degraded.

# Foster Powell
## The Astonishing Pedestrian

In the year 1764, not for any wager, Mr. Foster Powell undertook to walk fifty miles on the Bath road in seven hours, having gone the first ten miles in one hour, although encumbered with a great coat and leather breeches.

He visited several parts of Switzerland and France, and gained much praise there for his pedestrianism; but in the year 1773, he walked from London to York and back again, 400 miles, in five days and eighteen hours: this was his first match for a wager.

In 1787, he undertook to walk from Canterbury to London Bridge and back again, in twenty-four hours; this he accomplished to the astonishment of thousands of anxious spectators, who were assembled to witness the completion of his task.

In 1792, he determined to convince the world he could journey to York and back again in a shorter time then ever he had, though now at the advanced age of fifty-eight years. Accordingly he set out from Shoreditch Church to York Minster, and back again, which he completed in five days, fifteen hours and one quarter. On his return he was saluted with the loud huzzas of the astonished and anxious spectators.

Previous to this he undertook a journey to Canterbury, but, by unfortunately mistaking the road from Blackheath to London, he unavoidably lost the wager; yet he gained more money by this accident than all the journeys he accomplished; for his friends, feeling for the great disappointment he experienced, made a subscription, and collected for him a good present.

In person he was tall and thin, about five feet nine inches high, very strong downwards, well calculated for walking, and rather of a sallow complexion; in disposition he was mild and gentle, and possessed many valuable qualifications. In diet he was somewhat particular, as he preferred light food; he abstained from liquor, but on his journey made use of brandy, and when travelling, the delay he met with at the inns, for he had particular hours for taking refreshment, often chagrined him. No wonder, indeed, if, on this account, he had often lost his wagers. He allowed himself but five hours' rest, which took place from eleven o'clock at night.

In 1793, he was suddenly taken ill, and died on the 15th of April, at his apartments in New Inn, in rather indigent circumstances, for, notwithstanding his wonderful feats, and the means he had of attaining wealth, poverty was the constant companion of his travels through life, even to the hour of his death. The faculty attributed the cause of his sudden dissolution to the great exertions of his last journey to York, for being determined to complete it in less time than ever, he probably exceeded and forced his strength. In the afternoon of the 22nd, his remains were brought, according to his own request, to the burying ground of St. Faith, St. Paul's Churchyard. The funeral was, characteristically, a walking one, from New Inn, through Fleet Street, and up Ludgate Hill. 

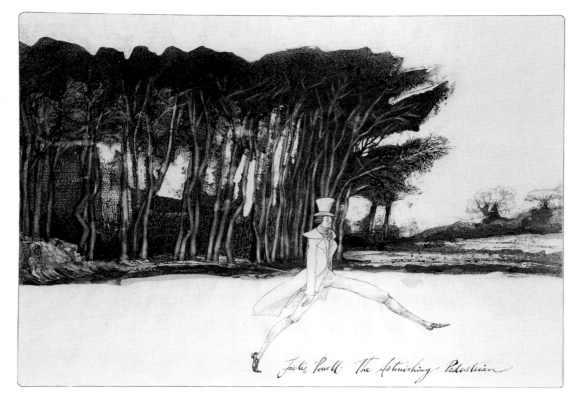

*Foster Powell: The Astonishing Pedestrian*

# Peter The Wild Boy
## Of the Woods of Hamelin

On the continent of Europe, the regions of which are interspersed with vast forests and uncultivated tracts, various individuals of the human species have at different times been discovered in a state no better than that of the brute creation. Most of these unfortunate beings were so completely brutalized as to be utter strangers to the faculty of speech and totally incapable of acquiring it – a fact which demonstrates how much man is indebted to the society of his fellow-creatures for many of the eminent advantages possessed by him over the other classes of animated nature.

One of the most singular of these human brutes was Peter the Wild Boy. He was found in the year 1725, in a wood near Hamelin, walking on his hands and feet, climbing trees like a squirrel, and feeding on grass and moss.

He appeared to have scarcely any ideas, was uneasy at being obliged to wear clothes, and could not be induced to lie on a bed, but sat and slept in a corner of the room, whence it was conjectured that he used to sleep in a tree for security against wild beasts.

Mr. Burgess of Oxford made further inquiries concerning Peter, and transmitted an account, which was in substance as follows:

Peter, in his youth, was very remarkable for his strength, which always appeared so much superior, that the stoutest young men were afraid to contend with him. When he was brought to England, he was particularly fond of raw flesh and bones, and was always dressed in fine clothes, of which he seemed not a little proud. He still retains his passion for finery; and if any person has anything smooth or shining in his dress, it soon attracts the notice of Peter, who shows his attention by stroking it. Gin is one of the most powerful means to persuade him to do anything with alacrity; hold up a glass of that liquor, and he will not fail to smile and raise his voice.

If he hears any music, he will clap his hands, and throw his head about in a wild frantic manner. He has a very quick sense of music, and will often repeat a tune after once hearing it. He understands everything that is said to him by his master and mistress. While I was with him, the farmer asked him several questions, which he answered rapidly, and not very distinctly, but sufficiently so as to be understood even by a stranger to his manner. I was told that when he first came into that part of the country, different methods were taken to teach him to read, and to instruct him in the principles of religion, but in vain. He learned nothing, nor did he show any feeling of the consciousness of a God.

Of the people who are about him, he is particularly attached to his master. He will often go out into the field with him and his men, and seems pleased to be employed in anything that can assist them. But he must always have some persons to direct his actions, as you may judge from the following circumstances. Peter was one day engaged with his master in filling a dung-cart. His master had occasion to go into the house, and left Peter to finish the work, which he soon accomplished. But as Peter must be employed, he saw no reason why he should not be as usefully employed in emptying the cart as he had before been in filling it.

On his master's return he found the cart nearly emptied again, and learned a lesson by it which he never afterwards neglected.

PETER — the wild boy from the woods of HAMELIN

# Ann Moore
## The Fasting Woman

About the beginning of 1807, residing then at Tutbury, a village in Staffordshire, Ann Moore first excited the public attention by declaring she could live without food. An assertion so repugnant to reason and nature, was of course rejected; she therefore offered to prove the truth of her statement by submitting to be watched for a considerable time.

When the watch had ended, she was removed to her own house, and Mr. Taylor published an account, declaring that she had lived for thirteen days without taking any food, liquid or solid. This account, so attested, was believed by numbers, who flocked to see her, and few visited her without leaving some proof of their credulity or pity. By this means she collected about £250.

In order to give additional weight to her case, she professed to be very religious; the Bible was laid on her bed, and here conversation was such as led the ignorant to imagine her to be a person of extraordinary piety. But his mask was thrown off whenever she was pressed too hard by pointed questions from those who still doubted. On such occasions she would vent such virulent language as would fully evince the absence of any religious principle in her.

Though the declaration of the persons who formerly watched her, in addition to her own assertions, had obtained considerable credit, yet there were many who thought her an impostor, and demanded that she should again be watched; this for some time she refused, and at length, most unwillingly she consented.

Her bed was filled with chaff, and the clothes examined in the presence of the committee. The watch entered on their office at two o'clock on Wednesday. She received the watchers with as much good manners as she was capable of, though she had been crying bitterly before they came.

At the end of seven days the public was informed that she had during that time taken no food whatever. Great confidence was now expressed by her advocates, that she would endure the ordeal with credit. But on the ninth day, she insisted on the watchers quitting the room, declaring that she was very ill, and that her daughter must be sent for. She was now greatly reduced, and it was thought that she could not live two hours longer, but after the watchers had left her, and the daughter admitted, the mother began to recover.

One remarkable circumstance was, that on Friday, the 30th April, after the watch broke up, she desired to take a solemn oath that she had not taken any food whatever. This she did in hope, notwithstanding all, still to impose upon the public. But as her clothes gave evidence against her, to her utter confusion, she was brought at last to make a full confession.

This juggler was committed to prison in February, 1816, for falsely collecting money under the pretence of charity. Since it is unknown what became of her, the name of Ann Moore is only remembered as that of an impostor of the vilest description. ⚹

Ann MOORE
The fasting woman

# Old Boots
## Of Ripon in Yorkshire

The real name of this very conspicuous personage it is impossible to ascertain: in his life-time he was known only by the significant appellation of Old Boots. He was, however, born about the year 1692, and for some length of time, filled the important office of boot-cleaner at an inn at Ripon in Yorkshire. He was a perfect lusus naturae; Dame Nature forming him in one of her freakish humours. He was blessed with such plenitude of nose and chin, and so tenderly endearing were they that they used to embrace each other; and by habit, he could hold a piece of money between them. Among the variety of human countenances, none perhaps ever excited more public curiosity than that of Old Boots. He invariably went into the rooms with a boot-jack and a pair of slippers; and the urbanity of his manners was always pleasing to the company, who frequently gave him money, on condition that he would hold it between his nose and chin; which request he always complied with, and bore off the treasure with great satisfaction. He was one of those fortunate beings who could daily accomplish that which thousands of persons are ineffectually striving all their lives to attain – he could 'make both ends meet'! He died in 1762, at the age of seventy.

OLD BOOTS
A well known character at Ripon in YORKSHIRE.

# Floram Marchand
## The Great Water-Spouter

In the summer of 1650, a Frenchman named Floram Marchand was brought over from Tours to London, who professed to be able to 'turn water into wine, and at his vomit render not only the tincture, but the strength and smell of several wines, and several waters.' Here – the trick and its cause being utterly unknown – he seems for a time to have gulled and astonished the public to no small extent, and to his great profit.

Before, however, the whole mystery was cleared up by two friends of Marchand, who had probably not received the share of the profits to which they thought themselves entitled. Their somewhat circumstantial account runs as follows.

'To prepare his body for so hard a task, before he makes his appearance on the stage, he takes a pill about the quantity of a hazel nut, confected with the gall of an heifer, and wheat flour baked. After which he drinks privately in his chamber four or five pints of luke-warm water, to take all the foulness and slime from his stomach, and to avoid that loathsome spectacle which otherwise would make thick the water, and offend the eye of the observer.

'In the first place he presents you with a pail of luke-warm water, and sixteen glasses in a basket, but you are to understand that every morning he boils two ounces of Brazil thin-sliced in three pints of running water, so long till the whole strength and colour of the Brazil is exhausted; of this he drinks half a pint in his private chamber before he comes on the stage.

'Before he presents himself to the spectators, he washes all his glasses in the best white-wine vinegar he can procure. Coming on the stage, he always washes his first glass, and rinses it two or three times, to take away the strength of the vinegar, that it may in no wise discolour the complexion of what is represented to be wine.

'At his first entrance, he drinks four and twenty glasses of luke-warm water, the first vomit he makes the water seems to be a deep claret: you are to observe that his gall-pill in the morning, and so many glasses of luke-warm water afterwards, will force him into a sudden capacity to vomit, which vomit upon so much warm water, is for the most part so violent on him, that he cannot forbear if he would.

'Having then made his essay on claret, he will bring forth claret and beer at once into several glasses; now you are to observe that the glass which appears to be claret is rinsed as before, but the beer glass not rinsed at all, but is still moist with the white-wine vinegar, and the first strength of the Brazil water being lost, it makes the water which he vomits up to be more of a pale colour, and much like our English beer.

He will then, in succession, bring up pale Burgundian wine, sack and finally white wine.

'It is also to be considered that he never comes on the stage (as he does sometimes three or four times in a day) but he first drinks the Brazil water, without which he can do nothing at all, for all that comes from him has a tincture of the red, and it only varies and alters according to the abundance of water which he takes, and the strength of the white-wine vinegar, in which all the glasses are washed.' ✳

# Matthew Lovat

## Who Crucified Himself

We shall in this chapter present our readers with some account of the crucifixion, which Matthew Lovat executed upon his own person, on the morning of the 19th of July, 1805. He was forty-six years of age when he committed this act of pious suicide.

Until the month of July, 1802, Matthew Lovat did nothing extraordinary. His life was regular and uniform; his habits were simple, and comfortable to his rank in society; nothing, in short, distinguished him but an extreme degree of devotion. He spoke on no other subjects than the affairs of the Church. Its festivals and fasts, with sermons, saints, etc., constituted the topics of his conversation. It was at this date, however, that, having shut himself up in his chamber, and making use of one of the tools belonging to his trade, he performed upon himself the most complete general amputation, and threw the parts of which he had deprived his person from his window into the street. It has never been precisely ascertained, what were the motives which induced him to this unnatural act. Some have supposed that he was impelled to it by the chagrin, with which he was seized, upon finding his love rejected by a girl of whom he had become enamoured; but is it not more reasonable to think, considering the known character of the man, that his timid conscience took the alarm of some little stirrings of the flesh against the spirit, had carried him to the resolution of freeing himself at once and for ever of so formidable an enemy? However this may be, Lovat, in meditating the execution of this barbarous operation, had also thought of the means of cure. He had mashed and prepared certain herbs, which the inhabitants of his village deemed efficacious in stemming the flow of blood from wounds, and provided himself with rags of old linen to make the application of his balsam, and what is surprising, these feeble means were attended with such success, that the cure was completed in a very short time, the patient neither experiencing any involuntary loss of urine, nor any difficulty in voiding it.

It was not possible that a deed of this nature could remain concealed. The whole village resounded with the fame of Matthew's exploit, and everybody expressed astonishment at his speedy cure without the aid of a professional person. But he himself had not anticipated the species of celebrity which the knowledge of his expert operation was to procure for him; and not being able to withstand the bitter jokes which all the inhabitants of the village, and particularly the young people, heaped upon him, he kept himself shut up in his house, from which he did not venture to stir for some time, not even to go to mass.

Eventually he came to the resolution of going to Venice. But scarcely was he established in this new abode, when ideas of crucifixion laid hold of him. He wrought a little every day in forming the instrument of his torture, and provided himself with the necessary articles of nails, ropes, bands, the crown of thorns, etc.

These cruel preparations being ended, Matthew proceeded to crown himself with thorns; of which two or three pierced the skin which covered the forehead. Next, with a white handkerchief bound round his loins and thighs, he covered the place formerly occupied by the parts of which he had deprived himself, leaving the rest of his body bare. Then, seating himself upon the cross, he took one of the nails destined for his hands, of which the point was smooth and sharp, and introducing it into the palm of the left, he drove it, by striking its head on the floor, until the half of it had appeared through the back of the hand. He now adjusted his feet to the bracket which had been prepared to receive them, the right over the left; and taking a nail five French inches and a half long, of which the point was also polished and sharp and placing it on the upper foot with his left hand, he drove it with a mallet which he held in his right, until it not only penetrated both his feet, but entering the hole prepared for it in the bracket, made its way so far in the tree of the cross as to fasten the victim firmly to it. He planted the third nail in his right hand as he had managed with regard to the left, and having bound himself by the middle to the perpendicular of the cross by a cord, which he had previously stretched under him, he set about inflicting the wound in the side with a cobbler's knife, which he had placed by him for this operation.

These bloody operations being concluded, it was now necessary, in order to complete the execution of the whole plan which he had conceived, that Matthew should exhibit himself upon the cross to the eyes of the public, and he realized this part of it in the following way. The cross was laid horizontally on the floor, its lower extremity resting upon the parapet of the window, which was very low; so, raising himself up by pressing upon the points of his fingers (for the nails did not allow him to use his whole hand either open or closed), he made several springs forward, until the portion of the cross which was protruded over the parapet, overbalancing what was within the chamber, the whole frame, with the poor fanatic upon, darted out at the window, and remained suspended outside of the house by the ropes which were secured to the beam in the inside. It was then eight o'clock in the morning. As soon as he was perceived, some humane people ran upstairs, disengaged him from the cross, and put him to bed.

It happened that Dr. Ruggieri, to whom we owe the above account, was called to the spot by some business connected with his profession. Having heard what had taken place, he instantly repaired to the lodgings of Lovat, to witness with his own eyes a fact which appeared to exceed all belief; and when he arrived there in company with the surgeon Paganoni, he actually beheld him wounded in the manner described. With the permission of the Director of Police of the Royal Canal, who had come to take cognizance of what had happened, Dr. Ruggieri caused the patient to be conveyed by water to the Imperial Clinical School, established at the Hospital of St. Luke and St. John, and entrusted to his care. During the passage the only thing he said was to his brother Angelo, who accompanied him in the boat, and was lamenting his extravagance, which was 'Alas! I am very unfortunate.'

He lay at the hospital for about a month, subjected to the most careful medical treatment, under which his wounds began gradually to heal. During the greater part of this time he hardly ever spoke. Always somber and shut up in himself, his eyes were almost constantly closed. 'I interrogated him several times,' says Dr. Ruggieri, 'relative to the motive which had induced him to crucify himself, and he always made me this answer, "The pride of man must be mortified, it must expire on the cross."'

Scarcely was he able to support in his hand the weight of a book, when he took the prayer-book, and read it all day long. On the first days of August, all his wounds were completely cured; and as he felt no pain or difficulty in moving his hands or feet, he expressed a wish to go out of the hospital, that he might not, as he said, eat the bread of idleness. This request being denied to him, he passed a whole day without taking any food; and finding that his clothes were kept from him, he set out one afternoon in his shirt, but was soon brought back by the servants. The Board of Police, being informed of the cure of this unhappy man, very wisely gave orders that he should be conveyed to the Lunatic Asylum, established at St. Servolo. Thither he was brought on 20th August, 1805.

# Jane Lewson

## An Eccentric Old Lady

Mrs. Lewson (commonly called Lady Lewson, from her very eccentric manner of dress) was born in the year 1700, in Essex Street in the Strand, of reputable parents of the name of Vaughan, and was married at an early age to Mr. Lewson, a wealthy gentleman, then living in the house in which she died. She became a widow at the age of twenty-six, having only one daughter living at the time. Mrs. Lewson being left by her husband in affluent circumstances, preferred to continue single, and remained so, although she had many suitors. When her daughter married, being left alone, she became fond of retirement, and rarely went out, or permitted the visits of any person. For the last thirty years of her life she kept no servant, except one old female, who died after a servitude of twenty years, and was succeeded by her grand-daughter, who marrying shortly after, was replaced by an old man, who attended the different houses in the square to go on errands, clean shoes, etc. Mrs. Lewson took this man into her house, and he acted as her steward, butler, cook and housemaid; and, with the exception of two old lap dogs and a cat, he was her only companion. The house she occupied was large, and elegantly furnished, but very ancient; the beds were kept constantly made, although they had not been slept in for about thirty years. Her apartment being only occasionally swept out, but never washed, the windows were so crusted with dirt that they hardly admitted a ray of light. She used to tell her acquaintance that, if the rooms were wetted, it might be the occasion of her catching cold; and as to cleaning the windows, she observed, that many accidents happened through that ridiculous practice: the glass might be broken, the person might be wounded, and the expense would fall upon her to repair them. A large garden in the rear of the house was the only thing she paid attention to; this was always kept in good order; and here, when the weather permitted, she enjoyed the air, or sometimes sat and read, of which she was particularly fond; or else chatted on times past, with any of the few remaining acquaintances whose visits she permitted. She seldom visited, except at a grocer's in the square, with whom she dealt. She had for many years survived every relative within many degrees of kindred. She was so partial to the fashions that prevailed in her youthful days, that she never changed the manner of her dress from that worn in the time of George I, being always decorated 'with ruffs, and cuffs, and fardingales, and things'.

She always wore powder, with a large tache made of horse hair, upon her head, over which the hair was turned up, and a cap over it which knotted under her chin, and three or four curls hanging down her neck; she generally wore silk gowns, and the train long, with a deep flounce all round; a very long waist, and very tightly laced up to her neck, round which was a kind of ruff or frill. The sleeves of her gown came down below the elbow, from each of which four or five large cuffs were attached; a large bonnet quite flat, high-heeled shoes, a large black silk cloak, trimmed round with lace, and a gold-headed cane, completed her every-day costume for the last eighty years, and in which she walked round the square.

She never washed herself, because those people who did so, she said, were always taking cold, or laying the foundation of some dreadful disorder; her method was to besmear her face and neck all over with hog's-lard, because that was soft and lubricating; and then, because she wanted a little colour on her cheeks, she used to bedaub them with rose pink!

Her manner of living was so methodical, that she would not drink her tea out of any other than a favourite cup. She was equally particular with respect to her knives, forks, plates, etc. At breakfast she arranged in a particular way the paraphernalia of the tea-table; at dinner, she also observed a general rule, and always sat in her favourite chair. She always enjoyed excellent health, assisted in regulating her house and never had, until a short time before her decease, an hour's illness. She entertained the greatest aversion to medicine; and what is remarkable, she cut two new teeth at the age of eighty-seven, and was never troubled with the tooth-ache. She lived in five reigns, and was supposed the most faithful living historian of her time, events of the year 1715 being fresh in her recollection. A few days previous to her death, an old lady, who was her neighbour, died suddenly, which had such an effect upon her, that she frequently said that her time was also come, and she should soon follow. She enjoyed all her faculties until that period, when she became weak, took to her bed and refused medical aid. Her conduct to her few distant relations was exceedingly capricious and she would never see any of them; and it was not until a few hours before her dissolution, that any alteration was observed in her temper.

She died on Tuesday, May 28th, 1816, at her house in Cold Bath Square at the advanced age of 116 and was buried in Bunhill-fields burying ground.

Jane LEWSON
An Eccentric Old Lady

Ralph STEADman

Henry LEMOINE
The Eccentric
Bookseller
and
Author

Henry Lemoine was born in Spitalfields in the memorable year of the unfortunate overthrow of Lisbon. At fourteen years of age he was apprenticed to a stationer and rag-merchant in Lamb Street, Spitalfields, who, though he dealt in books, had such an aversion to learning, that he was constantly ill-tempered whenever Lemoine was reading, which often happened in spite of his ill humour. Thus his servitude was enlivened by the pursuit of letters at stolen hours, and borrowed from the time of rest, when, with the assistance of a lamp fitted to a dark lanthorn, he contrived to read and digest some necessary works of history, poetry, arts and sciences.

In 1780 he began business in Bishopsgate churchyard; at this time he kept good company; the day was spent at his sky-covered shop in philosophical conversations, and reciprocal communication with some of the first characters; and the evenings, and even nights, in the orgies of youthful blood; yet amidst all this dissipation, he evinced some prudence in his choice of companions, which he always selected from situations better than his own. Saturday nights were particularly devoted to these irregularities, which he jocosely called 'borrowing an hour with the Lord', and some of these frolics sometimes assumed a very serious aspect.

As an indefatigable disseminator of literature he brought out a collection of Apparitional histories, prefaced by an ingenious argument, endeavouring to convince the world of the reality of 'the visits from the world of spirits.'

About this time he published the *Kentish Curate*, a narrative romance in four volumes, exhibiting some of the most depraved characters in life, but as they are properly hung out to view on the gibbet of reproach, their examples can do no harm.

Though condemned, by the harshness of his fate, to a daily dependence on his industry about the street and at sales, to pick up rare and uncommon books, he never so far complied with the wickedness of others as to assist in the publication or sale of improper books or prints.

He was one of the very best judges in England of old books, a professor of the French and German languages, an able commentator on the Jewish writings, an amiable and unaffected man, an enlightened companion. He ended his chequered life in St. Bartholomew's Hospital, April 30th, 1812, aged fifty-six years.

# Henry Jenkins

## The Modern Methuselah

Few countries can produce such numerous instances of extraordinary longevity as the British islands, which afford incontestable proof of the healthiness of their climate. Among these examples, the most remarkable is, perhaps, that of Henry Jenkins, who attained the patriarchal age of 169 years. The only account now extant of this venerable man is that given by Mrs. Ann Saville, who resided at Bolton, in Yorkshire, where Jenkins lived, and had frequent opportunities of seeing and conversing with him.

'When I came', says she, 'to live at Bolton, I was told several particulars of the great age of Henry Jenkins; but I believed little of the story for many years, till one day he coming to beg an alms, I desired him to tell me truly how old he was. He paused a little, and then said, that to the best of his remembrance, he was about 162, or 163; and I asked him, what kings he remembered? He said, Henry VIII. I asked him what public thing he could longest remember? He said, Flodden Field. I asked whether the king was there? He said, no, he was in France, and the Earl of Surrey was general. I asked him how old he might be then; he said, I believe I might be between ten and twelve; for, says he, I was sent to Northallerton with a horse-load of arrows, but they sent a bigger boy from thence to the army with them. All this agreed with the history of that time; for boys and arrows were then used, the Earl he named was general, and King Henry VIII was then at Tournay. And yet it is observable that this Jenkins could neither read nor write. He told me then too that he was butler to the Lord Conyers and remembered the Abbot of Fountains Abbey very well, before the dissolution of the monasteries. Henry Jenkins departed this life December 8th, 1670, at Ellerton-upon-Swale in Yorkshire. The battle of Flodden Field was fought September 9th, 1513, and he was twelve years old when Flodden Field was fought. So that this Henry Jenkins lived 169 years, viz. sixteen years longer than old Parr, and was, it is supposed, the oldest man born upon the ruins of the post-diluvian world.

'In the last century of his life he was a fisherman, and used to trade in the streams: his diet was coarse and sour, and towards the latter end of his days he begged up and down. He has sworn in Chancery, and other courts, to above 140 years' memory, and was often at the assizes at York, whither he generally went on foot; and I have heard some of the country gentlemen affirm, that he frequently swam in the rivers after he was past the age of 100 years. In the king's remembrancer's office in the Exchequer, is a record of a deposition in a cause by English bill, between Anthony Clark and Smirkson, taken 1665, at Kettering in Yorkshire, where Henry Jenkins, of Ellerton-upon-Swale, labourer, aged 157 years, was produced and deposed as a witness.'

About seventy years after his death a monument was erected at Bolton, by a subscription of the parishioners, to perpetuate the memory of this remarkable man. Upon it was engraved the following inscription:

'Blush not, marble, to rescue from oblivion the memory of Henry Jenkins, a person of obscure birth, but of a life truly memorable: for he was enriched with the goods of nature, if not of fortune, and happy in the duration, if not variety of his enjoyments: and though the partial world despised and disregarded his low and humble state, the equal eye of Providence beheld and blessed it with a patriarch's health and length of days, to teach mistaken man these blessings are entailed on temperance, a life of labour, and a mind at ease. He lived to the amazing age of 169: was interred here, December 16th, 1670, and had this justice done to his memory, 1743.'

Henry JENKINS

Who lived to be 169 years.

Ralph STEADman

The Famous Rope-Dancer

JACOB HALL
The Famous Rope-Dancer
Ralph STEADman

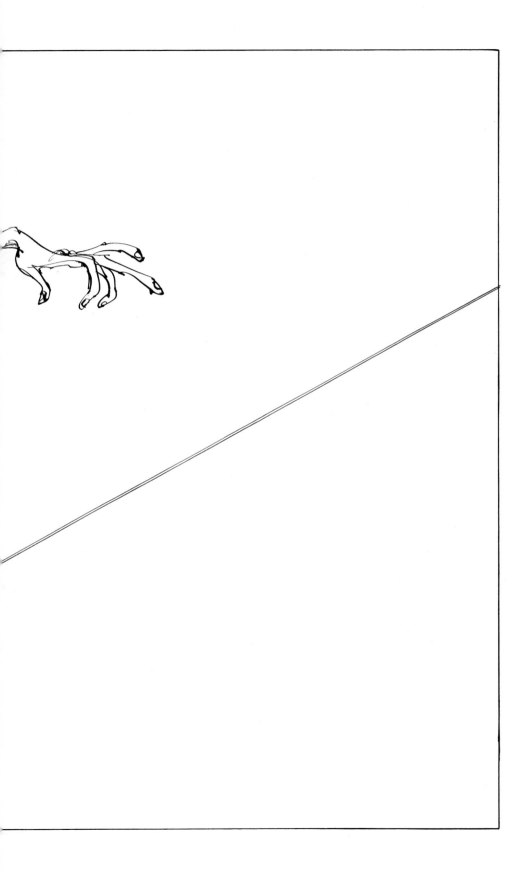

There was a symmetry and elegance, as well as strength and agility, in the person of Jacob Hall (*to be regarded overleaf*), which was much admired by the ladies, who regarded him as a due composition of Hercules and Adonis. The open-hearted Duchess of Cleveland was said to have been in love with this rope-dancer, and Goodman, the player, at the same time. The former received a salary from Her Grace.

Pepys has given a short account of Hall in his diary:

'21st September, 1668, Thence to Jacob Hall's dancing on the ropes, where I saw such action as I never saw before, and mightily worth seeing; and here took acquaintance with a fellow that carried me to a tavern, whither came the music of this booth, and by and by Jacob Hall himself, with whom I had a mind to speak, to hear whether he had ever any mischief by falls in his time. He told me, "Yes, many, but never to the breaking of a limb": he seems a mighty strong man.'

# Charles Domery
## The Remarkable Glutton

Charles Domery, a native of Benche, on the frontiers of Poland, at the age of twenty-one, was brought to the prison of Liverpool in February, 1799, having been a solider in the French service on board the *Hoche*, captured by the squadron under the command of Sir J.B. Warren, off Ireland.

He was one of nine brothers, who, with their father, were remarkable for the voraciousness of their appetites. They were all placed early in the army; and the peculiar craving for food with this young man began at thirteen years of age.

He was allowed two rations in the army, and by his earnings, or the indulgence of his comrades, procured an additional supply.

When in the camp, if bread or meat were scarce, he made up the deficiency by eating four or five pounds of grass daily; and in one year devoured 174 cats (not their skins) dead or alive; and says, he had several severe conflicts

Charles DOMERY
The Remarkable
GLUTTON

in the act of destroying them, by feeling the effect of their torments on his face and hands: sometimes he killed them before eating, but when very hungry, did not wait to perform this humane office.

Dogs and rats equally suffered from his merciless jaws; and if much pinched by famine, the entrails of animals indiscriminately became his prey. The above facts are attested by Picard, a respectable man, who was his comrade in the same regiment on board the *Hoche*, and who had often seen him feed on those animals.

When the ship on board of which he was had surrendered after an obstinate action, finding himself, as usual, hungry, and nothing else in his way but a man's leg, which was shot off, lying before him, he attacked it greedily, and was feeding heartily when a sailor snatched it from him, and threw it overboard.

While he was in prison, though plentifully supplied by eating the rations of ten men daily, he complained he had not the same quantity, nor indulged in eating so much as he used to do, when in France.

The eagerness with which he attacked his beef when his stomach was not gorged resembled the voracity of a hungry wolf, tearing off and swallowing it with canine greediness. When his throat was dry from continued exercise, he lubricated it by stripping off the grease of the candles between his teeth, which he generally finished at three mouthfuls, and wrapping the wick like a ball, string and all, sent it after at a swallow. On recapitulating the whole consumption of one day, it stands thus:

| | |
|---|---|
| Raw cow's udder .................... | 4 pounds |
| Raw beef ............................... | 10 |
| Candles ................................. | 2 |
| Total ..................................... | 16 pounds, besides |
| | five bottles of porter. |

From such a subject as this the heart naturally revolts, and we are happy in closing so disagreeable a biography. May future records never be stained with another so detestable a creature as Charles Domery – so appalling to every natural and civilized feeling, so degrading to the human character. There are numerous instances of voracity in existence, but none so revolting to humanity as this.

Ralph STEADman

# Guillaume De Nittis
## Who Tried to Eat Himself

So depressed was Guillaume de Nittis with nature, God and the deformities bestowed upon him, that he set about eating himself into shape. He got no further than eating his stump of a forearm before he was arrested and charged with disturbing the peace, indecent exposure and grievous bodily harm. He was placed in protective custody in the prison hospital, but became morose, uncooperative and refused to eat the prison food. He was placed in solitary confinement, and while there proceeded to eat off his left foot.

He was restrained and put into a strait-jacket for his own good but de Nittis managed to chew through the straps and release himself sufficiently to eat what he considered to be unsightly appendages of his form. The prison doctor succeeded in obtaining an explanation from the wretched creature who told him that God was such a poor sculptor that he was trying to help rectify the shameful state of affairs.

Told that he would surely die if he persisted with this gruesome habit, Guillaume replied that he would continue until only his teeth were left which were the only perfect thing in his body. Guillaume de Nittis died of shock a week later on July 4th, 1876, aged thirty-two years, exactly one hundred years after the American War of Independence, when he bit off his testicles to celebrate the event – which strikes the author as exceptionally weird.

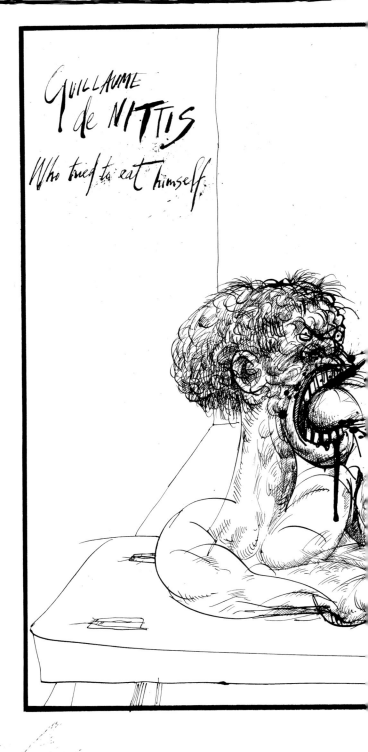

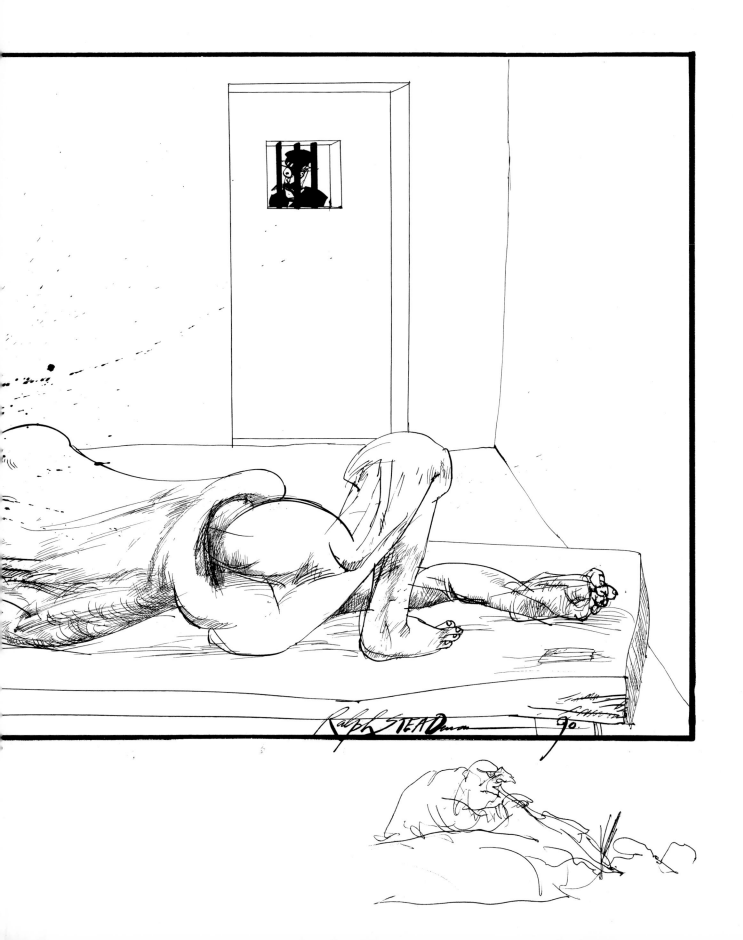

# Carl Unthan
## The Armless Fiddler

It wasn't merely that people were astonished at the fact that Carl Unthan could actually get a tune out of a violin with his feet but that he could play with such virtuosity.

When he plunged into a frenzy of complex solo flights from Brahms' Second Violin Concerto, accompanied by the Viennese Orchestra conducted by Johann Strauss the Younger, at the Dianasaal Concert Hall, the concentration was intense, his otherwise angelic face became demonic and the audience was spellbound. He won the admiration of music lovers on three continents.

Born on the 5th of April, 1848, in Sommerfeld, East Russia, Carl was a healthy, happy boy in spite of his handicap.

His father, a strict authoritarian, refused to allow anyone to feel sorry for the boy for fear that he would nurture self-pity. He insisted that the boy should not wear shoes and socks as he had a tendency to reach for things on his own with his feet. Gradually, he developed great dexterity and power in his lower regions. He also developed infinite patience. He taught himself to read and write by the time he was six. He learned to swim on his back and dress himself.

At the age of ten, he determined to learn to play the violin. Tying the instrument to a kitchen chair he took up the bow with his left foot and 'fingered' the strings with his toes.

By the time he was sixteen Carl was sent to the Conservatory to study musical theory and at twenty he gave his first concert. He has been known to change a broken string on stage in the middle of a performance to tumultuous applause. Travelling the world his act took on as much a vaudeville flavour as musical. He would light cigars, uncork bottles, cut cakes, shuffle cards and do sleight-of-foot tricks. Then he would play the violin, double on a cornet and finished off shooting a rifle at moving targets without missing once.

He married a singer, learned to type, gave lectures about his skills and the development of his limbs, saved a drowning woman in a film called *The Armless Man* and joined the army to perform for the soldiers.

Before his long and distinguished life was over he wrote his autobiography, in longfoot. As a violinist he may well have achieved greater eminence had he avoided the grinding vaudeville circuit. ✳

# Wybrand Lolkes

## The Dutch Dwarf

ybrand Lolkes was a native of Holland, and born at Jelst in West Friesland, in the year 1733, of parents in but indifferent circumstances, his father being a fisherman, who besides this most extraordinary little creature, had to support a family of seven other children, all of whom were of ordinary stature, as were both the father and mother. Wybrand Lolkes, at an early age, exhibited proofs of a taste for mechanism; and when of sufficient age, was, by the interest of some friends, placed with an eminent watch- and clock-maker at Amsterdam, to learn that business; he continued to serve this master for four years after the expiration of his apprenticeship, and then removed to Rotterdam, where he carried on the business of a watch-maker, on his own account, and where he first became acquainted, and afterwards married, the person who accompanied him to England. His trade of watch-maker, however, failing, he came to the resolution of exhibiting his person publicly as a show; and by attending the several Dutch fairs obtained a handsome competency. Impelled by curiosity and hope of gain, he came to England, and was visited at Harwich (where he first landed) by crowds of people; encouraged by this early success, he proceeded to London, and on applying to the late Mr Philip Astley, obtained an engagement at a weekly salary of five guineas. He first appeared at the Amphitheatre, Westminster Bridge, on Easter Monday, 1790, and continued to exhibit every evening during the whole season. He always was accompanied by his wife, who came on the stage with him hand in hand, but though he elevated his arm, she was compelled to stoop considerably to meet the proffered honour. At this time he was sixty years of age, measured only twenty-seven inches in height, and weighed exactly fifty-six pounds.

Mynheer Lolkes was a fond husband; he well knew the value of his partner, and repaid her care of him with the most fervent affection. He had by his wife three children, one of which, a son, lived to the age of twenty-three and was five feet seven inches in height.

This little man, notwithstanding his clumsy and awkward appearance, was remarkably agile, and possessed uncommon strength, and could with the greatest ease spring from the ground into a chair of ordinary height. He was rather of a morose temper and extremely vain of himself, and while discoursing in broken English was extremely dignified as he imagined. He continued in England but one season, and through the help of a good benefit, returned to his native country, with his pockets better furnished than when he left.

WYBRAND LOLKES
The Dutch Dwarf

# Eli Bowen "the legless wonder" and Charles Tripp "the armless wonder"

As friends, Charles Tripp and Eli Bowen were ideally suited, in both courage and application.

Bowen became known as 'the legless acrobat' who did tricks on a pole and Charles Tripp became known as 'the armless wonder' who, like the aforementioned Carl Unthan, could do most things with his feet that the rest of us rarely achieve with all our faculties and appendages.

The desire to succeed overcomes disability and an apparently helpless form breaks its physical bonds to achieve the impossible and still reach beyond. The Thalidomide generation demonstrated this without reservation, including particularly the parents and relatives who somehow found reserves of strength that simply do not exist in ordinary circumstances.

Eli BOWEN
"the legless WONDER"
and
Charles TRIPP
the armless WONDER

Charles Tripp was born on 6th July, 1855, in Woodstock, Canada, without arms, and Eli Bowen, some ten years earlier on 4th October, 1844, in Richland County, Ohio, without legs in spite of the fact that his mother had reared nine other perfectly normal children. Like all folk who were born with less or more than is normal, in Victorian times the only place they could really excel was in the circus; and Charles Tripp joined P.T. Barnum, the American showman spectacular, and travelled the world as what would then have been a 'novelty freak'. Finding Barnum in New York, he performed his tricks in front of the circus owner's desk and was hired on the spot.

He was just seventeen. He married in later life and lived on until 1939, aged eighty-four.

Eli Bowen began his career much earlier at the age of thirteen and became an exhibitionist on a wagon show, called Mayor Brown's Colosseum. He toured with many of the historic circuses and also travelled the world with the Greatest Show on Earth, in 1897.

He met Charles Tripp and they would do a double act together and devise tricks for two people which required only one pair of hands and one pair of legs. Eli had the same dislike for small boys as W.C. Fields, probably because he was often the butt of their jokes, just as Fields was always upstaged by them. Eli Bowen too married and raised a large healthy family in California.

A most popular act, the duo was the only one of its kind ever.

# St. Joseph of Copertino

## The Flying Friar

Guisseppe Desa of Copertino showed an early interest in religion, building his own corner altar in the family squat where he recited the rosary and litany at regular intervals night and day. It is claimed he had his first ecstasy looking heavenward with mouth open during school lessons and earned the nickname 'Open Mouth'.

In his late teens he attempted to enter a friary run by two of his relations, who resisted his application, considering him to be ignorant and alarming.

At last, in 1625, he became a cleric at a provincial chapter at Altamara, and here a strange thing happened. After mass he went to pray in a corner observed by the Nuns of St. Ligario. Suddenly, he levitated, shrieked and flew in the standing position onto the altar amid the burning candles and flowers. The nuns were horrified until he floated down to the church floor in the kneeling position, then spun around on his knees in exultation to the Blessed Virgin.

The levitations became more frequent and his fame spread. Wherever he went and wherever there was an icon or religious object, he would become enraptured and fly up towards it. When visiting the sick who had pictures of the Blessed Virgin above their beds he would leap over them and alight quite delicately on to the bedside table crowded with medicines and drinking vessels, never disturbing a single object.

Even the sight of nature gave Guisseppe cause to shriek with delight and thanksgiving, when he would leap into air and alight on a branch that would normally only support the weight of a sparrow. He would often return to his senses while still up the tree and wonder how he got there as he fell to earth.

He has been known to lift others with him, and heavy crosses constructed to be erected in high places he lifted with ease. Such accounts were disbelieved by many, save those who saw the occurrences or who themselves were borne aloft in states of great anxiety by one in a state of great ecstasy.

It is claimed that a lunatic nobleman was brought before Guisseppe tied to a chain to restrain him. The flying friar had untied him, grabbed the knight by his hair and rapturously dragged him aloft chanting incantations to the Holy Mother for at least fifteen minutes, curing him with what amounts to one of the earliest examples of shock therapy.

With such manifestations of supernatural powers, St. Joseph of Copertino, as he became known, converted Lutheran dukes to Roman Catholicism, and saw into the hearts and minds of doubting marchionesses, princes and admirals, leaving behind a confusion of fainting ladies, whom he found all through his life particularly repugnant.

He healed the sick, multiplied food, found lost objects and demonstrated the power of bilocation, that is, being in

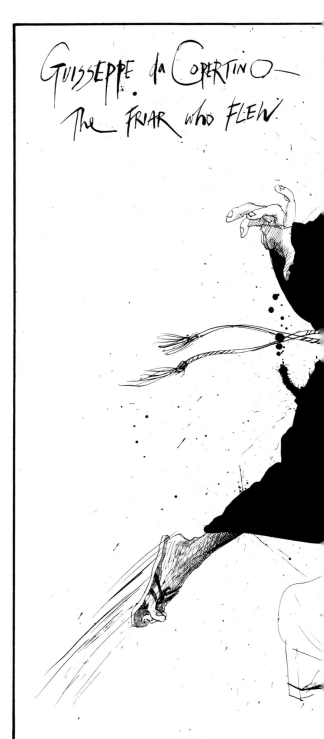

GUISSEPPE da COPERTINO—
The FRIAR who FLEW.

two places at the same time. He claims to have met the devil on many occasions and attacked him, invoking St. Francis, who emerged from his tomb to help.

The occasion of his death, which occurred after a month's feverish illness on 18th September, 1663, was equally weird. The day before he died he claimed he could hear God summoning him with a bell. He rose from his deathbed and flew out of his cell towards his chapel and, having received Extreme Unction, boomed in a huge voice in spite of a deathly weakness, 'Oh, what sounds of Paradise!' and the spirit left his body.

Whether his body then slumped on the floor like an old container whose job is done is not mentioned.

Whether such apparent miracles concerning saints are diabolic or divine has always been a sensitive matter for the Church, but often ecstasies are only achieved by such severe austerities and self-inflicted pain that they often suggest diabolic rather than divine intervention.

However, Joseph of Copertino was finally decreed a Saint on 16th July, 1767, after much deliberation and sifting of evidence before a tribunal called the Congregation of Sacred Rites, who try to tear the evidence to shreds.

# Alexis Vincent Charles Berbiguier
## The Demon Bottler

Ralph STEADman

The problem of demon containment and disposal has preoccupied priests, demonologists and holy sages since the dawn of time. Exorcism is an ancient practice. In Christianity it is performed by the simple linking of hands and in other religions more severe methods and even sacrifices are demanded. It is still considered to be an effective and believable way of drawing Satan out of a possessed person. Bottling was the common method of rendering a jinn and his power impotent. Such a bottler was Alexis Charles Berbiguier, the Scourge of Demons, who made the devil his *raison d'être*.

Berbiguier was born in Carpentras in the department of Vaucluse, in 1765. His mother would not breast-feed him and he was to be fed by wet nurse and the bottle. His health and stability of mind were affected, he was partially crippled and paranoiac, believing his life to be marked and persecuted. Rather than blame bad doctoring, his bruised mind believed only that demons were responsible for his condition and it was in bedrooms that demons found easy prey to absorb their wanton ways.

This made Berbiguier a morose and introspective brooder who would stay in his darkened room and see

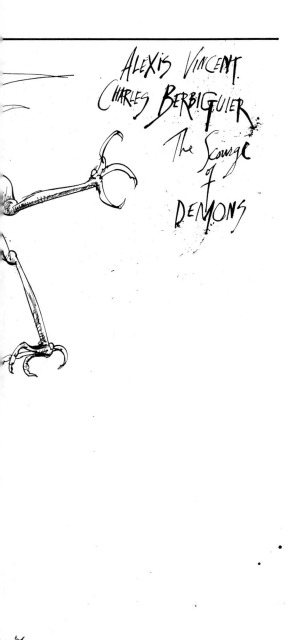

ALEXIS VINCENT.
CHARLES BERBIGUIER
The Scourge of
DEMONS

demons at bay, though he knew that demons often invaded his room in the form of fleas and lice. He found that they liked tobacco, which he would scatter about to intoxicate them, making it easy to sweep them into bottles and cork them in. His bed became a pin cushion. The pins, he claimed, pierced a wriggling goblin.

In 1821 the printer Gueffier published Berbiguier's Encyclopaedia of Demonolgy, called *Les Farfadets*, or *All Demons Are Not From the Other World*. It appeared in three volumes and Berbiguier gave himself the title of Scourge of Demons. Around a portrait of him are the symbols of his craft, the heart of an ox stuck with pins, crossed sticks of sulphur, aromatic plants and, in memoriam, a picture of his squirrel, Coco.

In the General Preface, Berbiguier writes:

'I have suffered much, and am still suffering. For twenty years demons, sorcerers and farfadets have not allowed me a moment's rest; everywhere they pursue me: in the town and country, in church and at home, and even in my bed. My head is sound, and no defect mars the good condition of my body. I am made in the image of our Saviour. Why, then, have I been chosen as the principal victim?'

All doctors are accused of being Satan's disciples and those that come disguised as fleas and lice enter a victim's body through the various orifices.

He suggested wild treatments for manifestations of possession, like trepanning to release the evil spirits out of lady who said she had a canary in her head. A surgeon pretended to operate to placate him but treated the woman by auto-suggestion.

Berbiguier became slovenly, filthy and unkempt, wandering the streets clutching a bottle to his chest which also supported his twisted neck made so by demons and evil spirits who attacked him daily. His back too was humped and twisted and he muttered to anyone who would listen the bottle contained the thousands of demons he had caught that very morning.

His condition worsened and he voluntarily entered a hospital back in his home town of Carpentras and died happily on 3rd December, 1854, certain that he would go to a place where no demon dare follow. His paranoid schizophrenia disappeared in the puff of a last breath and with it all the bottled demons he had spent a lifetime capturing. Only his books leave behind a detailed record of the processes and development of delusional hysteria. I have yet to find a copy by chance in some antiquarian bookshop. 

visions in his mirror, would suffer foul odours, and a mysterious injury was inflicted on Coco, his pet squirrel. Berbiguier was convinced now that demons were persecuting him and he began to address them through letters calling them excrements of the earth, execrable emissions and infernal powers. He called them Les Farfadets; and he was certain that most, if not all, women were demons who had been ravished in their sleep and enjoyed by the devil and his followers.

He waged war on all that was demonic and concocted broths of oxen hearts adorned with pins which kept the

# Charles Charlesworth

## Who Died of Old Age at the Age of Seven

The ageing process affects us all at different rates. Some people of fifty-three, like the esteemed author, look a mere thirty-five, with sparkling brown eyes, a handsome gait and the virility of a steam train. Others, like the author's friend Colin, look like little middle-aged men at twenty-one with middle-aged outlooks of set ways and planned futures. In women the former condition is common but women rarely suffer from the latter, being fired with the insatiable drive of ambition for either an independent and distinguished career in a still male-dominated world, or a home and seven children by the time they are thirty followed by an independent and distinguished career as a Cheltenham councillor or a public relations agent for Jonathan Cape, in later life.

No such luck for Charles Charlesworth, who was born on the 14th of March, 1829, in Stafford. At the age of four Charles had a beard and was sexually active.

In the final three years of his life his skin wrinkled, he developed varicose veins, shortness of breath, grey hair, senile dementia and incontinence. Some time in his seventh year he fainted and never gained consciousness.

The coroner returned a verdict of natural causes due to old age. ✳

# Claude Ambroise Seurat
## The Living Skeleton

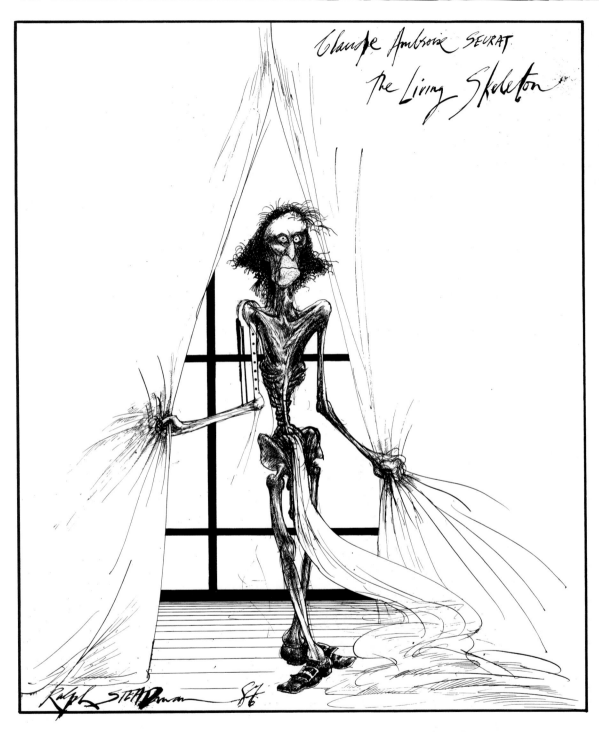

Claude Ambroise SEURAT
The Living Skeleton

Claude Ambroise Seurat, better known by the title of 'The Living Skeleton', was undoubtedly the greatest natural wonder of the period in which he lived. He was born at Troyes, in the department of Champaigne, on the 10th of April, 1797. His parents were respectable but poor, and unlike their son they both possessed a good constitution, and enjoyed robust health. At his birth there was nothing in his appearance that indicated disease, but in proportion as he grew in size, his flesh gradually wasted away. This remarkable decay continued till he arrived at manhood, when he attained his full stature, and his frame assumed the identical skeleton form which it ever afterwards retained. In France, his case excited great interest, and he was deemed quite a *lusus naturae*. While at Rouen, no less than fifteen hundred persons flocked in one day to see him.

It was in 1823 that he arrived in the British metropolis. Numerous descriptions of him appeared in the journals of the day. Perhaps the most graphic of the whole was that which Mr. Hone published in his *Every Day Book*, one of the most ingenious works of the time, full of curious, instructive, and amusing information, and now a universal library companion. A portion of his description I shall proceed to quote.

'On turning round, I was instantly riveted by his amazing emaciation; he seemed another "Lazarus, come forth" without his grave-clothes, and for a moment I was too consternated to observe more than his general appearance. My eye then first caught the arm as the most remarkable limb; from the shoulder to the elbow it is like an ivory German flute somewhat deepened in colour by age; it is not larger, and the skin is of that hue, and, not having a trace of muscle, it is as perfect a cylinder as a writing rule. Amazed by the wasted limbs, I was still more amazed by the extraordinary depression of the chest. Its indentation is similar to that which an over-careful mother makes in the pillowed surface of an infant's bed for its repose. Below the ribs, the trunk so immediately curves in, that the red band of the silk covering, though it is only loosely placed, seems a tourniquet to constrict the bowels within their prison-house, and the hip-bones, being of their natural size, the waist is like a wasp's. By this part of the frame we are reminded of some descriptions of the abstemious and Bedouin Arab of the desert, in whom it is said the abdomen seems to cling to the vertebrae. If the integument of the bowels can be called flesh, it is the only flesh on the body; for it seems to have wholly shrunk from the limbs.'

Such was the celebrated Living Skeleton seen by Mr. Hone and the thousands whom curiosity led to behold so remarkable a being. By his exhibition in this country he realized a little fortune with which he immediately retired to his native place, but did not live long to enjoy it. ➤✹

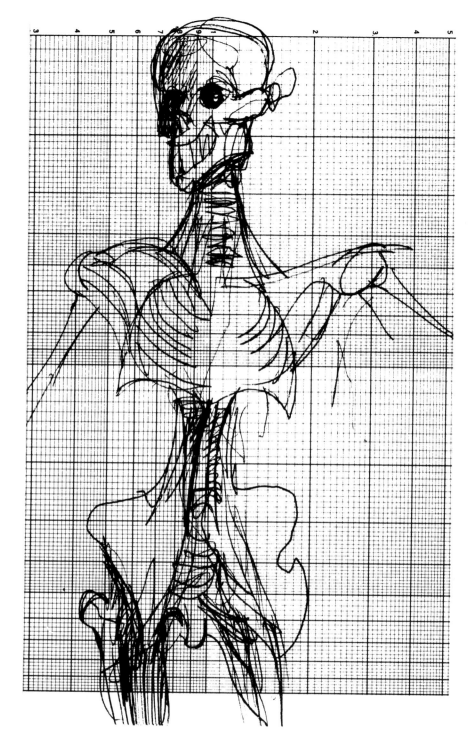

# Francis Trovillou
## The Horned Man

In the year 1598 a horned man was exhibited for a show, at Paris, two months successively, and from thence carried to Orleans, where he died soon after. His name was Francis Trovillou, of whom Fabritius, in his *Chirugical Observation*, gives the following description: 'He was of middle stature, a full body, bald, except in the hind part of the head, which had a few hairs upon it; his temper was morose, and his demeanour altogether rustic. He was born in a little village called Mézières, and bred up in the woods amongst the charcoal men. About the seventh year of his age he began to have a swelling in his forehead, so that in the course of about ten years he had a horn there as big as a man's finger-end, which afterwards did admit of that growth and increase, that when he came to be thirty-five years old this horn had both the bigness and resemblance of a ram's horn. It grew upon the midst of his forehead, and then bended backward as far as the coronal suture, where the other end of it did sometimes so stick in the skin that, to avoid much pain, he was constrained to cut off some part of the end of it. Whether this horn had its roots in the skin or forehead, I know not; but probably, being of that weight and bigness, it grew from the skull itself. Nor am I certain whether this man had any of those teeth which we call grinders. It was during this man's public exposure in Paris (saith Urstitious), in 1598, that I, in company with Dr. Jacobus Faeschius, the public professor of Basil, and Mr. Joannes Eckenstenius, did see and handle this horn.'

Francis TROVILLOU
The Horned Man.

# Baron D'Aguilar
## Of Starvation Farm

Baron D'Aguilar may justly be classed among the most singular characters of the age in which he lived. 'The elements were so mixed up in him' as to form a truly extraordinary combination of vice and virtue.

Having been left a widow in 1763, the baron, a few years afterwards, married the widow of Benjamin Mendes da Costa, Esq., who brought him a considerable fortune. During his first, and for some time after his second marriage, the baron lived in the highest style of fashion, in Broad Street Buildings. On the expiration of his lease he removed from Broad Street Buildings, renounced the character of a gentleman, became rude, slovenly, careless of his person and conduct, totally withdrawing himself from his family connexions and the society of the gay world.

Having relinquished the pursuits of a gentleman, the baron took it into his head to adopt those of the farmer, but his farming speculations he carried on in a manner peculiar to himself. His farmyard at Islington was a real curiosity of the kind. From the state in which the cattle were kept, it received the characteristic appellation of the 'Starvation Farm Yard'. These wretched animals, exhibiting the appearance of mere skin and bone, might be seen amidst heaps of dung and filth, some just ready to expire. The miserable situation of these animals, doomed to this state of living death, frequently excited the indignation of passengers, who would often assemble in crowds to hoot and pelt the baron, who generally appeared in a very mean and dirty dress. He never replied or took any notice of these unpleasant salutations, but availed himself of the first opportunity to make good his retreat. It is unknown for what purpose he kept the cattle, unless it were for amusement, as he derived from them little or no emolument. The only reason he ever assigned for stinting them to such a scanty allowance of food was, that they might know their master; for it should be observed, that he was very fond of homage.

And yet the baron was hardly destitute of charity, for his contributions to the poor were manifold and secret. He was also a liberal patron of public institutions, and though his cattle attested to the fact that he did not always feed the hungry, he was seldom backward at feeding the naked, frequently inviting home ragged and distressed females, for whom he provided comfortable garments. He had been known to take into his houses fatherless children, whom he occasionally made his servants, increasing their wages with their years.

The poor baron survived his wife six or seven years, and died in March 1802, leaving property of upwards of £200,000. His illness, an inflammation of the bowels, lasted seventeen days.

BARON D'AGUILAR
OF STARVATION
FARM

Ralph STEADman

# Daniel Lambert

## *Of Surprising Corpulency*

From the extraordinary bulk to which Daniel Lambert attained, the reader may naturally be disposed to inquire whether his parents were persons of remarkable dimensions. This was not the case, nor were any of his family inclined to corpulence, excepting an uncle and an aunt on the father's side, who were both very heavy.

It was only at the age of nineteen that he began to imagine that he should be a heavy man, but he had never perceived any indications that could lead him to suppose he should ever attain the excessive corpulence for which he was distinguished. He always possessed extraordinary muscular power, and at the time we are speaking of could lift great weights, and carry five-hundred-weight with ease. Had his habits been such as to bring his strength into action, he would have been an uncommonly powerful man.

About the year 1793, Mr. Lambert weighed thirty-two stone. Such were his feelings that he abhorred the very idea of exhibiting himself. None the less, though he lived exceedingly retired, the fame of his uncommon corpulence spread over the adjacent country to such a degree that he frequently found himself not a little incommoded by the curiosity of the people, which it was impossible to repress, and which they were continually devising the means of gratifying in spite of his reluctance.

Finding, at length, that he must either submit to be a close prisoner in his own house, or endure all the inconveniences without receiving any of the profits of an exhibition, he wisely strove to overcome his repugnance, and determined to visit the metropolis for that purpose. As it was impossible to procure a carriage large enough, he had a vehicle constructed expressly to convey him to London, where he arrived in 1806, and fixed his residence in Piccadilly.

His apartments there had more the air of a place of fashionable resort than that of an exhibition; and, as long as the town continued full, he was visited by a great deal of the best company.

After a residence of about five months in the metropolis, Mr. Lambert returned, in September 1806, to his native town, and from that period to his death he was chiefly engaged in travelling to the principal towns, where many thousands beheld with admiration his astonishing bulk.

He died on the 21st of June, 1809, and upon being weighed a few days before his death by the Caledonian balance, was found to be 52 stone 11 lb. in weight (14 lb. to the stone). It was found necessary to take down the window and wall of the room in which he lay to allow his coffin to be taken out.

Daniel LAMBERT
Of Surprising Corpulency

# Joanne Southcott

## An Extraordinary Fanatic

The first forty years of Joanna Southcott's life were spent in honest industry, without any other symptom of a disordered intellect than that she was zealously attached to the Methodist. The circumstances show how commonly delusion, blasphemy and madness are to be found in this country, and may lessen our wonder at the frenzy of Joanna and her followers.

Her own career began humbly, with prophecies concerning the weather, such as the popular English Almanacs contain; and threats concerning the fate of Europe, and the successes of the French, which were at that time the speculations of every newspaper, and of every alehouse politician. Some of these guesses chanced to be right.

She began to send books into the wold which were written partly in prose, partly in rhyme, all the verse and the greater part of the prose being delivered in the character of the Almighty! It is not possible to convey an adequate idea of this unparalleled and unimaginable nonsense. Her handwriting was illegibly bad; so that at last she found it convenient to receive orders to throw away the pen, and deliver her oracles orally; and the words flowed from her faster than her scribes could write them down. This may be well believed, for they were words and nothing else: a mere rhapsody of texts, vulgar interpretations – the vilest string of words in the vilest doggerel verse, which has no other connexion that what the vilest rhymes have suggested, she vented and her followers received as the dictates of immediate inspiration. A herd, however, was ready to devour this garbage as the bread of life. Among these early believers were three clergymen, one of them a man of fashion, fortune and noble family.

When she found that persons into whose society nothing else could have elevated her, listened to her with reverance, believed all her ravings, and supplied her with means and money to spread them abroad, it is not to be wondered at if she went on more boldly; the lucrativeness of the trade soon silencing all doubts of the truth of her inspiration.

She boldly asserted that she was the woman in the Revelations, who has the moon under her feet, and on her head a crown of twelve stars; the twelve stars being her twelve apostles, who with the second dozen of believers make up her four-and-twenty elders. In her visitation it was told her, that the angels rejoiced at her birth, because she was born to deliver both men and angels from the insults of the devil. The scheme of redemption, she said, was completed in her, and without her would be imperfect; by woman came the fall of man, by woman must come his redemption; woman plucked the evil fruit, and woman must pluck the good fruit; if the tree of knowledge was violated by Eve, the tree of life was reserved for Joanna.

This frenzy would have been speedily cured in Spain; bread and water, a solitary cell, and a little wholesome discipline, are specifics in such cases. Mark the difference in England. No bishop interferes; she therefore boldly asserted that she had the full consent of the bishops to declare that her call was from God, because, having been called upon to disprove it, they kept silent. She, who was used to earn her daily bread by daily labour, was taken into the houses of her wealthy believers, regarded as the most blessed among women, carried from one part of England to another, and treated everywhere with reverence little less than idolatry.

65

# Daniel Cuerton

## And His Astonishing Feats

This extraordinary character was born in Old Street, St. Lake's, and was by trade a ladies' shoemaker. For the last sixteen years he maintained himself by keeping an old iron shop in St. James' Street, near Grosvenor Square, and about four or five years before his death, he removed to John Street, Goodge Street, Tottenham Court Road, where he closed his earthly career, in the year 1803, aged fifty-four years. He weighed about eighteen stone, horseman's weight; was very broad across the shoulders, chest and back, had short, fat, thick thighs and was about five feet six inches high. Notwithstanding he was very fat he was remarkably active. I shall enumerate here some of the most astonishing feats of this man: he would take a glass or pot up with his elbows, put his hand under his arm-pits, and in this way drink his beer, punch, etc., and if anyone would pay for the pot, he would in this position, with his elbows, hammer a

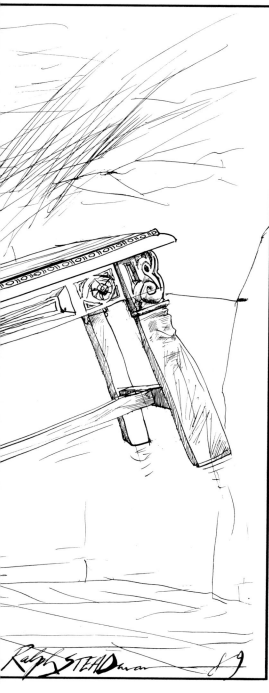

applied again at the same place, would measure round him and three other stout men, being four persons in the whole. How he did this none could tell, but it seemed he had an art of drawing his bowels up to his chest, and greatly swelling himself at pleasure. He would sit down on the ground, with his hands tied behind him, and bear a stout man across each shoulder, and one on his back, with a boy on top; in all four persons, besides himself; in this posture he would get up very nimbly, actively dance every step of a quick hornpipe, and whistle it himself all the time, for the space of ten or fifteen minutes. With his hands bound behind him, he would, without any aid, raise a large mahogany table with his fore teeth, that would dine twelve people on, balance it steadily, and with it break the ceiling, if desired, all to pieces. This remarkable man was well known by the free-masons at the west end of London, and for several years belonged to the Lodge No. 8, held at the King's Arms coffee-house, Lower Brook Street, Grosvenor Square. He was a very generous man, ever ready to assist the poor, unfortunate and distressed, with his purse, victuals, clothes, etc., and was always a ready advocate, and the first subscriber to a poor person's petition, when he was satisfied the person was a deserving object, whether man or woman. In the latter part of his time, he became much reduced in his circumstances, occasioned by many heavy losses in trade.

Poor Cuerton, in the days of his adversity, through extreme modesty, was always studious to conceal his distress, and whenever his situation was brought into question, his usual reply would be, he had known better days, and he did not like to be troublesome to anybody. He latterly contracted the baneful habit of drinking a great quantity of the juniper juice; this he made his constant beverage, the first thing in the morning, and the last at night. He used formerly to drink a great deal of porter, and eat very heartily, particularly at supper. He died almost in want, yet he had a great desire, when near his end, of being buried as a free-mason; but that society paid no attention to his request, although his widow made it known to them. He was a hearty, merry, good-natured companion, when he had health and money, and has paid many a reckoning for strangers, rather than hear any quarrelling or disputes, in the house where he happened to be. He never went to church or any place of worship, for several years past, as he was deaf, but it was always remarked, he could hear very well at a public house. He had been the constant promoter of greasy chins, and full bowls of punch, and used to enjoy them in an uncommon manner.

quart or pint pot together, as if it had been flattened with a large hammer. He could appear the largest or the smallest man across the chest in the company, if there were twenty persons present, and put on the coat of a boy of fourteen years of age, and it would apparently fit him. Such an astonishing way had he of compressing himself, that he would measure round under the arm-pits, with three handkerchiefs tied together, and yet the same measure,

# Barbara Urselin

## The Hairy-Faced Woman

This remarkable monstrosity was born at Augsburg, in High Germany, in the year 1629. Her face and hands are represented to have been hairy all over. Her aspect resembled that of a monkey. She had a very long and large spreading beard, the hair of which hung loose and flowing, like the hair of the head. She seems to have acquired some skill in playing on the organ and harpsichord.

A certain Michael Vanbeck married this frightful creature, on purpose to carry her about for a show. When she died is uncertain, but she was still living in 1668, when a Mr. John Bulfinch records that he saw her in Ratcliffe Highway, and 'was satisfied she was a woman'.

There are three portraits of her extant – one by Isaac Brunn, taken in 1653, and another by Gaywood, of five years later date. And now another, by the persistent recorder of all that is weird – the author.

# Eve Fleigen
## Who Lived on the Smell of Flowers

Eve Fleigen, or Veigen, was a native of the Duchy of
Cleve, in Germany. She is said to have lived long
upon no other nourishment than the smell of flowers.
Under one of the extant portraits of her are the following
lines:

> 'Twas I that pray'd I never might eat more,
> 'Cause my step-mother grutched me my food;
> Whether on flowers I fed, as I had store,
> Or on a dew that every morning stood
> Like honey on my lips, if I had lips,
>   full seventeen year,
> This is a truth, if you the truth will hear.

This story may keep company with Pliny's relation of the
Astomi, a people in East India, who have no mouths, are
supported by the smell of roots, flowers and wild apples;
and with that of the Chinese virgins, who are said to
conceive by smelling at a rose.

Yet this legend has a fine poetical sentiment underlying
it. Has there not for all of us been a time when our heart
was so full of spring that –

> It seem'd awhile that bounteous Heaven
> Nought else for man's support had given
> But sky, and trees, and flowers.

What?

# Elizabeth Woodcock
## Who Was Buried in Snow Nearly Eight Days

On Saturday, February 2nd, 1799, Elizabeth Woodcock was returning to Impington from Cambridge market. It was a very inclement, stormy night and snow began to accumulate so rapidly that, when Chesterton bell rang at eight o'clock, she was completely enclosed and hemmed in by it. Her imprisonment was now complete, for she was incapable of making any effectual attempt to extricate herself, and in addition to her fatigue and cold, her clothes were stiffened by the frost. Resigning herself, therefore, calmly to the necessity of her bad situation, she sat awaiting the dawn of the following day. Early the next morning she distinctly heard the ringing of a bell in one of the villages at a small distance. Her mind was now turned to the thoughts of her preservation, and busied itself in concerting expedients. She broke off a branch of the bush, which was close to her, and with it thrust her handkerchief through the hole, and hung it as a signal of distress upon one of the uppermost twigs that remained uncovered.

She had perfectly distinguished the alternations of day and night; heard the bells of her own and some neighbouring villages several different times. She recollected having pulled out her snuff-box and taking two pinches of snuff; but she felt so little gratification that she never repeated it. A common observer would have imagined the irritation arising from the snuff would have been peculiarly grateful to her, and that, being deprived of all other comforts, she would have solaced herself with those which the box afforded till the contents of it were exhausted. She frequently shouted out, in hopes that her vociferations reaching the ears of any that chanced to pass that way, they might be drawn to the spot where she was; but the snow so far prevented the transmission of her voice, that no one heard her.

When the period of her seclusion approached to a termination, and a thaw took place on the Friday after the commencement of her misfortune, she felt uncommonly faint and languid. But, fortunately, that Sunday, 10th February, Joseph Muncey, a young farmer, noticed a coloured handkerchief, hanging upon the tops of the twigs. He walked up to the place and heard a sound issue from it, similar to that of a person breathing hard and with difficulty. He looked in a saw a female figure, whom he recognized to be the identical woman who had been so long missing. He laid her gently in the carriage, covered her over with blankets, and conveyed her, without delay or interruption, to her own house.

Mr. Okes, a surgeon, first saw her. She spoke to him with a voice tolerably strong, but rather hoarse; her hands and arms were sodden, but not very cold, though her legs and feet were, and the latter in a great measure mortified. She was immediately put to bed, and weak broth given her occasionally. From the time of her being lost she had eaten only snow. She was so disturbed with company that Mr. Okes had little hopes of her recovery.

By the 27th all but one great toe had necessarily been removed, but by April 17th her sores were free from slough, and daily lessened; her appetite tolerably good, and her general health began to amend; she felt herself nonetheless to be very uncomfortable, and, in fact, her prospect was most miserable; for, though her life was saved, the mutilated state in which she was left was almost worse than death itself.

An account of her providential preservation was published at Cambridge in two parts. The first by the Rev. Mr. Holme, minister of her parish; the second by her surgeon, Mr. Thomas Verney Okes: the book was published for her benefit, and went through two editions.

This unfortunate woman closed a lingering existence on July 13th, 1799, and we are sorry to add, that too frequent indulgence of spirituous liquors was supposed to have been the cause both of the accident and its fatal consequences. ⚹

# Thomas Hills Everitt

## The Enormous Baby

This prodigious child, an extraordinary instance of the sudden and rapid increase of the human body, was born on 7th February, 1779. His father, a mould-paper maker, conducted the paper-mills by the side of Enfield Marsh, and was about thirty-six years of age; the mother was forty-two, but neither of the parents was remarkable for either size or stature. Thomas was their fifth child, and the eldest of the three living in 1780 was twelve years old, and rather small of his age; but the paternal grandfather was of a size larger than ordinary. They had another son of uncommon size, who died of the measles in January 1774, at the age of fifteen months.

Thomas was not remarkably large when born, but began, when six weeks old, to grow apace, and attained a most extraordinary size. At the age of nine months and two weeks, his dimensions were taken by Mr. Sherwen, an ingenious surgeon residing at Enfield, and compared with those of a lusty boy seven years old. The result was as follows:

| | Dimensions of the child. | Of the boy. |
|---|---|---|
| | Inches. | Inches. |
| Girth round the wrist ......................... | 6¾ | 4¾ |
| Ditto above the elbow ........................ | 8½ | 6¼ |
| Ditto of the leg near the ankle ........... | 9¾ | 6¼ |
| Ditto of the calf of the leg ................. | 12 | 9 |
| Ditto round the thigh ........................ | 18 | 12¾ |
| Ditto round the small of the back ..... | 24 | 22 |
| Ditto under the arm-pits and across the breast ........................... | 22¾ | 24 |

Mr. Sherwen who, in November 1779, transmitted the above account to Mr. Planta, secretary of the Royal Society, added that he should have been glad to have given the solid contents of animal substance, but was prevented by the vulgar prejudice entertained by the mother against weighing children. He could therefore only say that, when she exposed to view his legs, thighs and broad back, it was impossible to be impressed with any other idea than that of seeing a young giant. His weight was, however, guessed at nine stone, and his height at this period was three feet one inch and a quarter.

The child was soon afterwards conveyed to the house of a relation in Great Turnstile, Holborn, but the confined situation had such an effect on his health that it was found necessary to carry him back to his native air. His extraordinary size tempted his parents to remove him again to the metropolis, and to exhibit him to the public. His dimensions, as stated in the hand-bills distributed at the place of exhibition, and under a picture of Mrs. Everitt and her son, published in January 1780, from which the annexed print is copied, were taken when he was eleven months old. His height was then three feet three inches; his girth round the breast two feet six inches; the loins, three feet one inch; the thigh, one foot ten inches; the leg, one foot two inches; the arm, eleven inches and a half; the wrist, nine inches.

He was well proportioned all over, and subsisted entirely on the breast. His countenance was comely, but had rather more expression than is usual at his age, and was exceedingly pleasing, from his being uncommonly good-tempered. He had very fine hair, pure skin, free from any blemish, was extremely lively, and had a bright clear eye. His head was rather smaller in proportion than his other parts. From these circumstances Mr. Sherwen ventured to prognosticate that he was as likely to arrive at maturity, accidental disease excepted, as any child he ever saw. This opinion might, undoubtedly, have been well founded, notwithstanding the child's death, which took place about the middle of 1780, before he had attained the age of eighteen months. ✳

# Joseph Capper
## The Enemy of Flies

By his great quickness and industry, Mr. Joseph Capper at length amassed a sum sufficient to decline all business whatever, and therefore resolved to retire from the bustle of life. For several days he walked about the vicinity of London searching for lodgings, without being able to please himself. However, being one day much fatigued, he called at The Horns, Kennington, took a chop, spent the day, and asked for a bed in his usual blunt manner. When he was answered in the same churlish style by the landlord, that he could not have one, Mr. Capper resolved to stop, if he could, all his life, to plague the growling fellow, and refused to retire. After some altercation, however, he was accommodated with a bed, and never slept out of it for twenty-five years. During that time he made no agreement for lodging or eating, but wished to be considered a customer only for the day.

Soon after Mr. Townsend became landlord of The Horns he applied to the old man for a temporary loan: 'I wish', said he, 'to serve you, Townsend, you seem an industrious fellow; but how is it to be done, Mr. Townsend? I have sworn never to lend, I must therefore give it thee,' which he accordingly did the following day. Mr. Townsend proved grateful for this mark of liberality, and never ceased to administer to him every comfort the house would afford; and, what was, perhaps, more gratifying to the old man, he indulged him in his eccentricities.

His manner of living was so methodical, that he would not drink his tea out of any other than a favourite cup. In winter and summer he rose at the same hour, and when the mornings were dark, he was so accustomed to the house, that he walked about the apartments without the assistance of any light. At breakfast he arranged, in a peculiar way, all the paraphernalia of the tea-table. In the parlour he kept his favourite chair, and there he would often amuse himself with satirising the customers or the landlord. It was his maxim never to join in general conversation, but to interrupt it whenever he could say anything ill-natured.

Mr. Capper was elected steward of the parlour fire, and if any persons were daring enough to put a poker in it without his permission, they stood a fair chance of feeling the weight of his cane. In summer-time a favourite diversion of his was killing flies in the parlour with his cane; but as he was sensible of the ill opinion this would produce among the bystanders, he would with great ingenuity introduce a story about the rascality of all Frenchmen, 'whom', says he, 'I hate and detest, and would knock down just the same as these flies.' This was the signal for attack, and presently the killed and wounded were scattered about in all quarters of the room.

This truly eccentric character lived to the age of seventy-seven, in excellent health, and it was not until the Tuesday morning before his decease that a visible alteration was perceived in him.

The remains of the old gentleman were deposited in Aldgate church-yard, where his deceased sister was likewise laid.

# Thomas Hudson

## Remarkable for his Misfortunes

Hudson was a native of Leeds in Yorkshire, and in the earlier part of his life, filled a respectable situation as clerk in a government office in London, while in this employment, he came into possession of a considerable fortune by the death of an aunt; upon which, he retired into Staffordshire, where he remained for some years. Unfortunately he became a part to the celebrated South Sea scheme and lost his whole fortune in that disastrous project.

Misfortune now became his intimate companion – the news of the failure of his darling scheme arrived at the time when he had to witness the decease of an affectionate wife. These severe reverses were too much for him: he left his favourite residence in a state of bankruptcy, and made the best of his way to London. From this period he became in a manner insane; and Tom of Ten Thousand (as he used to call himself) was like Poor Joe – all alone!

The peculiarity of his dress and the deformity of his figure attracted particular notice: wrapped in a rug, and supported by a crutch, without either shoes or stockings, did this poor creature perambulate, even in the coldest weather, the Chelsea fields, craving help.

After many years of misery, death took this 'son of misfortune' from his earthly troubles, in the year 1767, at a very advanced age. ✳

# Deacon François De Paris
## Of Numerous Austerities

Some people seem destined from birth to have a catatonic effect on the lives of others no matter how short their own lives may have been.

François of Paris, the revered Deacon, was born on 3rd June, 1690, and was buried behind the High Altar of the Church of St. Medard at the northern end of the Avenue des Gobelins in May 1727. Formerly a cemetery and now a garden, it became a shrine for the Deacon's many followers. The Deacon himself was a Catholic who followed the teachings of Cornelius Jansen, a man bitterly opposed by the Jesuits who considered his teachings to be heretical.

Cornelius Jansen (1585-1638) was bishop of Ypres in Flanders. He believed in denying freedom of human will because of its natural perverseness and compulsive desire to be bad. An individual must resist divine grace for God would choose whom He pleased to love Him by total "conversion". Only through the Roman Church, he claimed, could the human soul find a personal relationship with God, though the movement was condemned by several popes who considered the severity of his teachings to damage the Church's unity.

His followers were called Jansenists and the Deacon François subjected himself to so many austerities in

Jansen's name that he died prematurely in 1727.

The day he died an unspecified miracle is supposed to have happened, which became the first of many in the churchyard of St. Medard, of a weird and sickly kind but nevertheless steeped in religious fervor and in good faith, that the blind shall see, the lame walk and the diseased be made whole.

At Lourdes, where only a simple faith is considered to be sufficient, at the tomb of the Deacon of Paris, fanatical behavior, blatant madness and extreme and tasteless weirdness would appear to be the style. But it seems cures were effected without, in some cases, even visiting the tomb in person. Cancers and malignant growths disappeared, supported by doctors' testimonies, though Professor Charcot, one of Freud's tutors at the Saltpetrière in Paris and a distinguished hypnotherapist in his own right, was not impressed.

A conversion to Jansenism brought about a phenomenal change in those who accepted the beliefs wholeheartedly.

One such, M. Fontaine, from the court of Louis XV, found his legs waste and the muscles turn to jelly, to be followed by an uncontrollable desire to revolve on one foot at a dinner party. He then demanded a devotional book and proceeded to read it aloud while still spinning at high speed – for an hour. His other foot rose up and described a circle, lowered only to increase speed and reach an incredible sixty turns a minute.

For six months, morning and afternoon, M. Fontaine rotated for an hour. His austerities increased and for eighteen days he gargled with strong vinegar, reducing the back of this throat to a raw and tender minefield of pain.

Indeed, these fits of rotating convulsions were common to all who became followers of Jansenism, or more particularly of the Deacon of Paris, as they paid homage to

his tomb and went into violent convulsive spins, standing on their heads, their hands, arching their backs and adopting quite indecent postures. They became known as the *Convulsionnaires*.

The Convulsionnaires had people in attendance (every movement seems to attract administrative staff) to help in the weirdest manifestations of the phenomenon. They would help to dress a woman in a long sheet tied at the ankles for the sake of decency – but some claimed Divine intervention kept these sheets and the women's dresses in place even though they were not tied.

Guides were present to steer curious visitors and potential followers around the cemetery explaining the hideous goings-on and the total madness they were witness to. They explained that it was God Almighty's power healing by way of these strange activities (which by any stretch of the imagination were cruel, insane and downright suicidal). Suffering and pain, it was claimed, are transformed into pleasure and delight in God's name on the spot.

Women and children up to twenty-five years of age in various states of sickness from lameness, deformity, sores and cancerous growths were being belabored about their bodies by assistants brandishing heavy hammers, lumps of wood and iron pestles. Blocks of stone were thumped down on to prostrate bodies showing no apparent distress. Nipples were gripped by fire tongs, then drawn and twisted. Sharp swords and metal shafts were prodded with great violence into the flesh of the possessed by the fiendish upholders of the faith. None of the abused showed any signs of pain.

The guides promised worse to come. Human Salamanders, Sore Suckers and Eaters of Ordure.

Suckers of Sores were considered to be divinely blessed. Applying "relics" of the Deacon of Paris to the suppurating wounds of victims presented to

Being beaten with huge PESTLES Gabrielle asks for a good HAMMERING

The tons shovels around a breast trick.

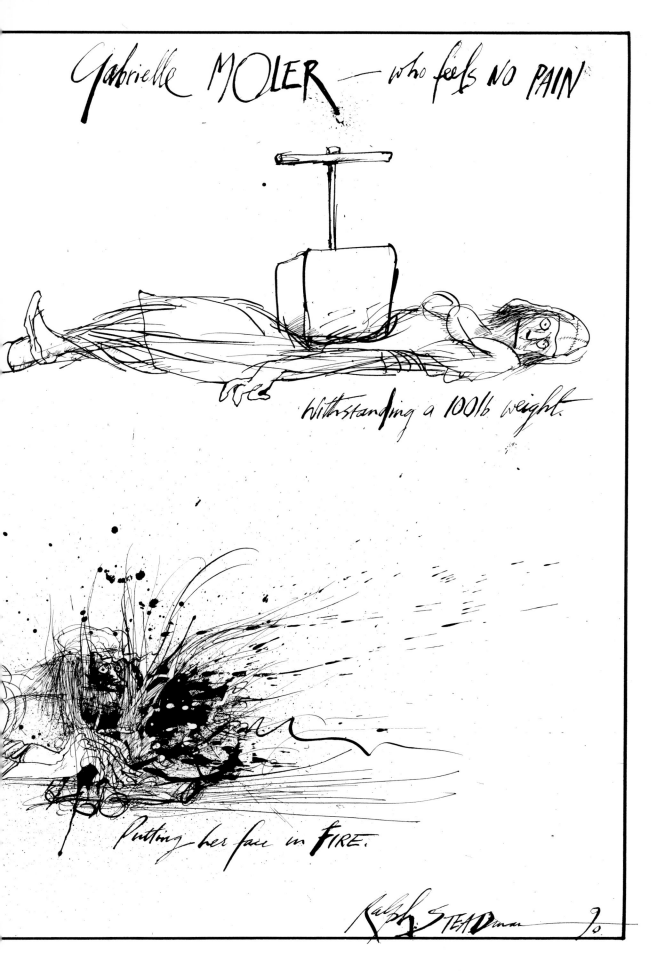

Gabrielle MOLER — who feels NO PAIN

Withstanding a 100lb weight.

Putting her face in FIRE.

Ralph STEADman

them, they proceeded to lick cancerous surfaces and suck pus out of deep, infected wounds and swallow the ghastly substance in the name of God and His overwhelming goodness. Furthermore they boiled the dirty bandages from these ulcerous sores, then drank the water.

Pale emaciated children, near to death, were brought before the possessed hags, who wallowed in the prospect of sucking away anything that festered, crying to the skies that the Lord was pleased to remove all these weaknesses from the face of earth.

When a sore was just too gross for even the Convulsionnaires to look at, let alone suck, they would cry out for strength from their Savior to help them, then set about the gruesome task with a renewed will and a frenzy.

The sight of a respected Parisian lawyer, M. le Paige, among such phantasmagorial behavior is perhaps an even stranger sight until you realize that he is there in his capacity as official voyeur to study the behavior of the Eater of Ordure, a young girl of eighteen or nineteen years of age: a Convulsionnaire of one year's standing, and one-time fastidious advocate of cleanliness until she felt the desire to subject herself to severe tests. She lived on bread and water for a time and then for nine days on a spoonful of ox bile once a day.

For the next month she ate only human excrement to cure what she described as a violent pain in her right side around her rib cage.

For 21 days her sole diet had been a pound of excrement and urine per day. This was verified by the lawyer, M. le Paige, who measured out her portions. Sometimes diluted – sometimes boiled. Occasionally she added chimney soot, nail clippings and slops.

She had a rosy complexion, robust good health and a jolly personality. She would then vomit and present a rooted onlooker with a glass of fresh milk. This, it was claimed, proved the presence of God's will upon her putrid activities since it was seen that such a transformation of contradictory substances was demonstrated as if it were a miracle.

Other Convulsionnaires, like *Gabrielle Moler*, subjected themselves to a severe grilling over hot coals and would apparently feel no pain. Some threw themselves into spiritual exercises of a more normal kind – jumping in the air and falling onto mattresses, rolling their eyes and twisting their heads, drooling their tongues like imbeciles, protruding their bellies suggestively and holding their breath until they fainted. Some would cry, whistle, bark and crow like animals, tumble about and lie in a crucified position, declaring prophecies while being pummeled with hammers and heavy objects. This they would do in front of patients who stood or lay depending on their condition, awaiting the miracle cure.

The Convulsionnaires

Gabrielle Moler excelled in her austerities. She allowed herself to be poked with rods and swords, and pummeled with massive stones without apparent bruising or marking.

Using specially sharpened shovels, strong heavy men would attempt to cut her shoulders off from above and, worse, allow four obviously willing bruisers to attempt to sever a breast using four shovels from four directions. All to no avail. Not a mark appeared on her body. Paradoxically, she would then be taken behind a screen to be examined discreetly by a committee of ladies to see if any damage had been inflicted, as though decency and decorum prevailed during these excessive demonstrations. The same treatment was inflicted on her throat but nothing would cut her. These willing gentlemen pummeled her like fiends a hundred times and still she asked for more. God was with her throughout and not even a tear appeared in her shift, ample proof that God was protecting her modesty also. The finale would be a fire test. Gabrielle would kneel in front of a massive fire and poke her head right inside the flames for a good fifteen minutes. On withdrawing her head not a sign of singeing was seen and she would ceremoniously take out a burning ember and eat it.

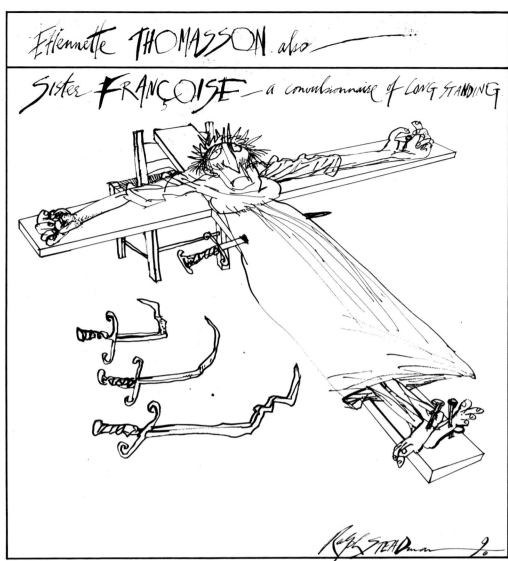

The antics of another, *Maria Sonnet*, seems no less intense. She would lie across two iron stools and allow a fire to be built around her middle to no apparent effect. Alternatively, she would stick her stockinged feet inside a brazier and, as she withdrew them, her stockings fell away in charred pieces, leaving her feet pristine and unmarked.

Due to complaints made about this sensational and ludicrous behavior, the cemetery of St. Medard was closed in 1732 by the authorities and the Convulsionnaires went underground.

Crucifixions became common and in 1759 a French philosopher, Charles Marie La Condamine, managed to witness an actual crucifixion of *Sister Françoise*, who was first subjected to a severe beating with chains by a zealous priest, Father Cottu, and various lay assistants. Sister Françoise was clutching a crucifix relic of the Deacon of Paris in an ecstatic trance and she then allowed herself to be laid over a cross supported by a chair and have three inch square nails driven through her hands and feet.

It is reported that attempts were made to pierce her side with swords which bent under pressure. However, this is surely open to questions, since if nails could pierce her hands how is it possible that swords could not pierce her side? The author is of the opinion that they did, and she survived after being propped up against a wall for three hours at a time – it happened more than once – which she followed with a drink of vinegar and cinders.

Even on her deathbed the maniac Father Cottu insisted on giving her a "good hammering" against the wishes of a physician present at her bedside. While they were arguing, Sister Françoise had a final convulsion and expired. "Thank God for that," sighed the physician.

Another group, the Fareinists from the little village of Farein, near Lyon, performed some antics, crucifixions, etc., but mercifully, their religious attitudes failed to win followers and their movement faded into history along with the Jansenist Convulsionnaires, though a movement is still believed to exist in Holland. Diseased manifestations of similar human stupidity and religious fanaticism do from time to time emerge, fuelled by the desire to believe in something greater than man's own spirit, which is forever in danger of being submerged beneath the heaving waters of a fevered mind. ✳

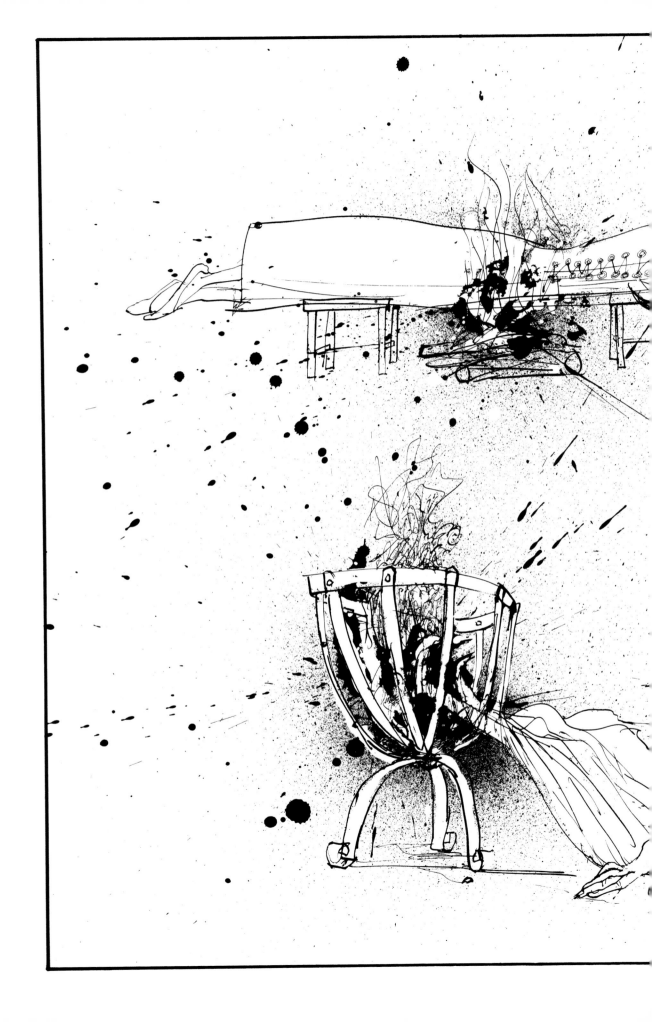

Maria SONNET

Fearless in FIRE.

Ralph STEADman

# Louise Clement

## Born with one eye

To be born with perhaps only one arm or one leg is barely startling, but this must be the only time in history that a human being was born with only one eye, not even on one side but right in the middle of the forehead. Such a girl was born to a French couple in Tourcoing in northern France.

In every other respect she was quite normal – as normal as one can be considering that, in order to accommodate a median eye, the structure of the head and maybe the brain would have undergone a fundamental change as the foetus developed in the womb.

Only in Greek mythology is such an aberration described, in the form of three storm gods: Brontes (Thunder), Steropes (Lightning) and Arges (the Thunder Bolt) – the three Cyclopes.

In Homer's *Odyssey* they forge the thunderbolts of Zeus and together with the Titans: ancestors of men and inventors of the arts and magic, and the Centimanes (the 'hundred-handed'): Coltus, the Furious; Gyges, the Big-limbed, and Briareus, the Vigorous – they represented the powerful forces of nature.

Little Louise, however, was blessed with none of these forces to protect her, though she may have enjoyed for a short time the wisdom of insight possessed by those with 'the third eye' in supernatural mythology. She lived to be only fifteen and would probably have died of grief and anguish and conceivably a clarity of vision, which would be considered far too great a shock for the human body to survive.

# Fakir Agastiya Of Bengal

## Who Kept his Arm in the Air for Ten Years

FAKIR AGASTIYA of BENGAL Kept his ARM in the air for 10 YEARS

The Fakirs of India are distinguished by their attempts to demonstrate their resistance to pain and privation. Some have been frauds and some have shown remarkable powers of mind over matter, demonstrating that all pleasure and pain is 'Maya' or illusion.

At the end of the nineteenth century Fakir Agastiya of Bengal proved the mental control he possessed over his body by raising his left arm above his head and leaving it in that position until he died in 1912. Gradually, the blood circulation diminished to almost nothing and rendered the arm completely numb and rigid. Even the joint locked, for Agastiya was laid to rest with his arm in the same position. The only poetic touch to an otherwise pointless exercise was the decision of a bird to nest in the palm of his hand.

Whether the accumulating bird-lime set solid over the years and helped to support his arm is unknown and open to after-dinner speculation.

# Joseph Pujol
## Le Pétomane

Of all the weird and curious people, perhaps the most famous of all is Le Pétomane (*The Fartomaniac, delineated on the previous pages*).

Everyone has heard of him and he is included in many a book of eccentrics. We all laugh about him because we all do what he does, the high, the low, the newborn and the inveterate boozer, the embarrassed and the silent, the loud and the clear, the toilet pipe-smokers and the room-clearers. Everyone does it just as surely as we all breathe through our noses.

But no one does it like Le Pétomane did it. His real name was Joseph Pujol. He was born in Marseille on 1st June, 1857, at 13 rue des Incurables, in itself an address worthy of a round of applause.

As a boy he discovered that if he completely submerged himself in a bath, water entered his body through his back passage, but he did not know until later that he could also control its intake and its ejection by using his stomach muscles and dilating or expanding his sphincter. He found he could also do it with air and with a little practice modulate the tone and speed of expulsion, giving him an instrument of rare musicality and panache. The sounds were so effective that it ceased to be a cause for embarrassment and became a favourite display of histrionics among his friends.

Eventually, he was persuaded to give a public performance, which offended the audience until a titter from someone of a coarser sensibility opened the floodgates and dissipated any further embarrassment. He was a great success and played to full houses in southern France, from Marseille to Clermont-Ferrand.

In 1892, he auditioned for the Moulin Rouge in Paris and was hired. Toulouse-Lautrec was at his most prolific at the time, and at least one drawing exists of Le Pétomane at work. The coarser he was, the better the Moulin patrons loved it. At will he could demonstrate the dulcet tones of a farting nun, the disarming rasp of a cab horse fed on barley oats and beer, or the regal trump of a member of any royal family in Europe.

He could imitate thunder, ripping fabric, rifle shots and a lion's roar without the slightest discomfort of smell for the audience, save that of the audience's own efforts common in such a basic establishment. He wrote farmyard poetry and accompanied his descriptions with a continuous background assortment of musical flatulence.

For decorum's sake he wore a smart outfit of red tailcoat, white butterfly tie, shiny black shoes over black socks and black satin breeches. He wore a moustache like all Frenchmen of the period and neatly barbered hair.

He varied his art with inserted tubes through which he smoked cigarettes, sucked drinks and played 'La Marseillaise' on a flute – just. He was earning more at the height of his success than Sarah Bernhardt, whom he could also imitate, but due to a row with the proprietor, M. Oller, he stormed out and violated his contract, for which he was sued. Oller then hired a female farter, Angèle Thiebeau, who turned out to be a fraud with a pair of bellows in her knickerbockers. Pujol sued her for plagiarism and fraud. Though she did establish that it still required skill to manipulate mechanical gadgets, Pujol won his case but did not pursue his court action.

Only one other lady of the time reached the prominence and skill to match the art of Le Pétomane. She called herself La Mère Alexandre and she effected a lady-like patter to attract a mixed audience ranging from children to white-haired old men. In the best possible taste she rattled off her impersonations of nuns, government officials, kings, queens, priests and regimental sergeant majors, finishing up with her *tour de force*, the relief of Mafeking.

Joseph Pujol continued to perform along with the whole family, who displayed other talents, and travelled through Europe and Africa playing to packed houses.

He continued until World War I but retired after his sons suffered severed injuries which broke his spirit if not his wind. He became a baker and biscuit maker. He was offered a large sum of money for his body after his death which he declined and he lived until 1945 aged eighty-eight. His famous last words were a nine-note blast of 'The Blue Danube' from his rear-end, provoking laughter around his deathbed. ✳

Le Pétomane

# The Wonderful Two-Headed Girl

As late as 1869 the wonderful two-headed girl was still on exhibition in New England. She sang duets by herself. She had a great advantage over the rest of her sex, for she never had to stop talking to eat, and when she was not eating she kept both tongues going at once. She had a lover who was in a quandary, because at one and the same moment she accepted him with one mouth and rejected him with the other. He knew not which to believe. He wished to sue for a breach of promise, but his was a hopeless experiment, because only half of the girl had been guilty of the breach. This girl had two heads, four arms, and four legs, but only one body, and she (or they) was (or were) seventeen years old.

Now was she her own sister?

Was she twins?

Or having but one body (and consequently but one heart), was she strictly but one person?

If the above-named young man had married her, would he have been guilty of bigamy?

The double girl had only one name, and passed for one girl – but when she talked back and forth with herself with her two mouths was she soliloquising?

Did she expect to have one vote or two?

Had she the same opinions as herself on all subjects, or did she differ sometimes?

Would she have felt insulted if she were to spit in her own face?

Just at this point the author feels compelled to drop this investigation, for it is rather too tangled for him.

# Miss Atkinson
## The Wonderful Pig-Faced Lady

Another story of world-wide fame deserves to be related in this worthy book. There can be few persons who have not heard of the celebrated Pig-Faced Lady, whose history, whether mythical or not, is common to several European languages, and is generally related in the following manner. A newly married lady of rank and fashion, being annoyed by the importunities of a wretched beggar-woman, accompanied by a dirty, squalling child, exclaimed – 'Take away your nasty pig, I shall not give you anything!' Whereupon the enraged mendicant, with a bitter imprecation, related – 'May your own child, when it is born, be more like a pig than mine!' And, accordingly, shortly afterwards the lady gave birth to a child, in which the beggar's unfortunate malediction was impartially fulfilled. It was a girl perfectly, nay, beautifully formed in every respect, save that its face, some say its whole head, exactly resembled that of a pig. This strange child thrived apace, and in course of time grew to be a woman, giving the unhappy parents great trouble and affliction; not only by its disgusting features alone, but also by its hoggish manners in general, much easier, at the present day, to be imagined than minutely described. The fond and wealthy parents, however, paid every attention to this hideous creature, their only child. Its voracious and indelicate appetite was appeased by the coarsest food of a hog, placed in a silver trough. To the waiting maid, who attended on the creature, risking the savage snaps of its beastly jaws, and enduring the horrible grunts and squeaks of its discordant voice, a small fortune had to be paid in annual wages, yet seldom could a person be obtained to fill the disagreeable situation longer than a month. A still greater perplexity ever troubled the unfortunate parents, namely, as to what would become of the wretched creature after their decease. Counsel learned in the law were consulted, who advised that the Pig-Faced Lady should be immediately married, the father, besides giving a handsome dowry in hand to the happy, or perhaps unhappy, bridegroom, he should be termed, settling a handsome annuity on the intrepid husband, for as long as she should live. But experience proving that after the first introduction, the boldest fortune-hunters declined any further acquaintance with her, another course was suggested. This was for the parents to found a hospital, the trustees of which were to be bound to protect and cherish the Pig-Faced damsel, until her death relieved them from the unpleasing guardianship. And thus it is that, after long and careful researches on the printed and legendary histories of Pig-Faced ladies, the writer has always found them wanting either a husband or a waiting maid, or connected with the founding of a hospital.

# Dulle Griet
## A Character in a Bruegel Painting

Ralph Steadman after the Looting Woman from the "Dulle Griet" by BRUEGEL

The Story of Dulle Griet, nicknamed 'Mad Meg', was passed down through generations of Flemish children who were told that she was an angry Giantess who led an army of fierce Flemish housewives into battle against the forces of Hell.

She captured the imagination of Pieter Bruegel the Elder who painted her storming across a battlefield of hellish specters and women aroused and battling with the demons of their nightmares. She is portrayed carrying a vast s word and looting as she goes. Later she became the inspiration for Berthold Brecht's *Mother Courage*, who followed the armies of Napoleon, wheeling and dealing her way through war and waiting on the perimeters of battlefields, like a vulture, to rifle the pockets of fallen soldiers, but who on occasions displayed the glimmer of a heart of gold. ✳

# Henry Constantine Jennings

## The Remarkable Virtuoso

This gentleman was descended of one of the first families in England, by the female line coming direct from George Duke of Clarence, brother to Edward IV and Richard III, Kings of England. The Countess of Salisbury beheaded for treason in the reign of Henry VIII was the daughter of the Duke of Clarence, and besides Cardinal Pole had several children; from one of which Mr. Jennings traced his pedigree.

He embarked in early life with a considerable fortune, which he greatly impaired through a vitiated taste for the fine arts; in which he never was outdone by any competitor. In the way of curiosities nothing came amiss to him; paintings, prints, fossils, minerals, shells, bronzes, carvings in ivory and wood, cameos, intaglios, miniatures, etc., of every description, graced his antique old-fashioned cabinets. On one occasion he had the temerity to give one thousand guineas for a representation of Alcibiades' dog, in marble, from which circumstance for many years after, he went by the name of 'Dog Jennings', though it appeared Mr. Jennings was not altogether in the wrong, as the dog was afterwards disposed of, at a considerable profit on the first purchase: some years since, Mr. Jennings acquired an addition to his fortune, by the demise of a friend, who left him a considerable income on condition of his adding the name of Nowell to his surname; but though he adopted the addition, he never was called by any other than the name of Jennings.

His mode of living kept pace with his other singularities: he was abstemious to a degree; and with respect to exercise, he was not only a great advocate for it, but practiced it to an extent scarcely credible, for upwards of half a century.

He possessed a long and ponderous wooden instrument, capped with lead at both ends; before bedtime, he exercised himself with this formidable weapon, until he acquired a comfortable warmth, which enabled him to retire to rest with a genial glow. In the morning, he got up between seven and eight o'clock; and, in his own express words, 'flourishing his broad sword exactly three hundred times; I then', adds he, 'mount my chaise horse, composed of leather, and inflated with wind like a pair of bellows, on which I take exactly one thousand gallops!' He then retired to enjoy, what always appeared to everyone, a most miserable and uncomfortable breakfast.

Had this gentleman possessed the revenue of a prince, it would have been inadequate to the eager desire he had to purchase the multitude of curiosities that were daily brought him from all quarters of the town; but what with one bargain, and what with another, he was fain at last to bargain for a room in the state-house of the King's Bench; where he removed himself, with his ark of curiosities, about the year 1816, and yet so much was he possessed of the true *mania* of virtue, that he would rather be deprived of liberty at the age of eighty, than part with one of his precious gems to procure his enlargement. At the time of his confinement, Mr. Jennings received full eight hundred pounds a year from some plantations he owned in the West Indies, which he never could be prevailed on to mortgage or otherwise encumber; and at the time of his death, had a case before the House of Lords, wherein he laid claim to a barony and considerable estate in right of descent and inheritance from one of his family.

The fate of Mr. Jennings has been eminently singular, and the flux and reflux, the ever-varying ebbs and flows of his fortune appear so strange as to be almost paradoxical. At an early period of life we behold him mingling in the crowd of wealthy pilgrims, who repaired to Italy about half a century ago, to pay their devotions at the shrine of taste and virtue. After keeping company with foreign princes and princesses he associates with the first nobility in his native country, and then by a fatal reverse, spends some years of his life, partly within the walls of a provincial, and partly of a town gaol. Recovering as if by magic, from his embarrassments, we next behold him emerging above the horizon of distress, and throwing away a second fortune at Newmarket, where he became the dupe of titled and untitled jockeys.

Sudden and inevitable ruin now seems to overtake him, and he is apparently lost for ever; but lo! in the course of a very short period, he once more revisits the circles of fashion, and sits enthroned in a temple, surrounded by the most rare and brilliant productions of nature, with pictures, and statues, and gems, and shells, and books, and goddesses, perpetually before his eyes! Again the scene changes: the wand of some envious necromancer seems to be waved over his venerable head; and the acquisitions of ages, the wreck of his estates, everything most precious in his eyes; his very 'household gods', are all seized by the unholy hands of vile bailiffs. He himself, after languishing for two or three years in a prison, at length dies unheeded, unattended, and almost unknown, within the purlieus of the King's Bench, in the year 1818.

Jennings, even in death, determined to prove singular: abhorring the idea of his corpse being consigned to the cold earth, he resolved to have recourse to the ancient rite of cremation. This was a circumstance so generally known, that his neighbours supposed he had an oven within his house, for the express purpose of reducing his body to ashes.

HENRY
CONSTANTINE
JENNINGS
The
Remarkable
Virtuoso

# Neville Vadio
## The Blind Caricaturist

Neville Vadio, the blind caricaturist, was claimed by many to be a greater draughtsman than Rembrandt. They justified their claim by saying that Vadio draws as he does purely by feel and touch, exploring the contours of a face he is about to interpret with extraordinarily sensitive fingers. If he could see as well, they said, his work would indeed be in the forefront of the art of all time.

As it was he fumbled his ideas onto paper, attempting to capture, through his groping fingers, what his 'inner eye' imagined. Very few people ever caught even so much as a glimpse of his work, for no sooner had he finished a drawing than he would destroy it, feeling that since he couldn't see the result of his efforts himself, neither should anyone else.

It is, therefore, difficult to ascertain if there was any merit in the work at all, or whether it was merely the spurious boast of a few who would seek to profit from the unfortunate man's unproven talent by deceit.

NEVILLE VADIO, the blind Caricaturist — who relied on touch and FEEL to draw - Ralph STEADman